VICTORY EVERY DAY

Walking with God in the Green Zone

Erik S. Cooper, M.A., LFMT

Troy Wehmeyer

ERIK&TROY
PUBLISHING

Ogallala, NE

Cover design & illustrations by Drake Sauer

Author photo by: Drake Sauer

Editing and interior layout by Carla F. Blowey

All scripture passages from the New International Version Bible (NIV)

Library of Congress Control Number: 2016906557

Published July, 2016

ISBN: 978-0-692-67305-8
ISBN: 0-692-67305-9

DEDICATION

We dedicate this book to those who are looking for
"victory every day" in their walk with Jesus Christ.

CONTENTS

FOREWORD

You will have trouble. Jesus guarantees it. In John 16:33, He says it clearly, "In this world you will have trouble." Psychologist, M. Scott Peck agrees as he tells us, "Life is difficult." I've been in pastoral ministry for about two decades now and one thing I can attest to is that they're right. Life is hard. Even those who come from strong families or have financial means struggle. Loss. Death. Disappointment. Betrayal. Neglect. If you've never experienced it, you can be certain that one day you will – probably sooner than later.

Jesus' promise that we'll have trouble is sandwiched with two other promises. He first is "In me, you may have peace." The second is "I have overcome the world." No matter what trouble we face, we don't have to be afraid. We don't have to falter. And, we don't have to lose.

Erik and Troy have made a lofty promise with the title "Victory Every Day". Trouble will come our way, but in Jesus we will not be overcome by it. The character traits from the Timeless Twenty Toolkit© in *Victory Every Day* won't remove all your troubles but they will help you navigate them with more peace and greater victory. To be sure, your peace will still be challenged and your victory will often appear tenuous but victory really is yours for the taking every day. The biblical principles in this book will help you find it, hold it and enjoy it.

The first step in the peace and victory over this world that Jesus offers is found in taking a step toward Him. Just as we have to choose to walk in forgiveness, self-control, hope or any of the Timeless Twenty character tools found in this guide, we won't enjoy the peace and victory Jesus offers us until we choose to walk with Him. And, from that moment on, we must choose to remain and abide in Him.

The reason we have trouble…the reason life is difficult, is because sin has entered the world as well as our hearts. In some way we have created our own pain through our own choices, and in many ways our pain has been handed to us by the choice of others. While tomorrow can most certainly be different if you choose, there is one thing that first must be done with the pain of yesterday and today.

Like so many, you may have learned to respond to any shame, guilt or anger that you feel by changing the subject, stuffing it down or moving on as quickly as possible. As you read through this book, you will certainly experience some of these emotions and feelings. While no one wants to experience them, let me suggest that these feelings aren't bad or wrong. View them instead as a warning light on your dashboard that indicates God is showing you there's something "under the hood" that needs to be dealt with.

To fully enjoy the freedom, peace and life of the "Green Zone" that Erik and Troy offer for your future, you must first put to rest the pain, brokenness and sin of yesterday. Shortly after Jesus had left this earth, one of his followers by the name of Peter said the following about Jesus: "There is no other name under heaven given to mankind by which we must be saved" (Acts 4:12).

There is one way to deal with the failures and pain of the past once and for all. It is to bring it all to the cross of Jesus Christ.. Understanding what was done to us, why it was done or even why we did something is tremendously helpful. But the only way it can really be paid for and completely settled is by bringing it to Jesus through faith.

The first steps are to admit that we've sinned, confess to God what we've done, and to ask Jesus to make us whole. If you haven't done so already, consider beginning your journey to victory by asking Jesus to take your sin and guide you through this life. Ask Him to take your life and heart and to lead you into wholeness and peace. Then ask Him to take you by the hand and show you how to live in that victory every day.

So as the warning indicators of negative feelings flash on in your heart and mind, take it as God's prompting that there's some work that He wants to do. Pause for a moment consider why you're feeling what you're feeling. If the cause is something you've done, all that needs to be done is to take that action to the cross. Tell God that you realize what you've done and ask Him to forgive you. Then, walk in the truth that "if we confess our sins, he is faithful and just and will forgive us our sins and purify us from all unrighteousness" (1 John 1:19).

If you have thoughts of something that was done to you, take it to the cross. Remember, forgiveness is not saying something is OK that wasn't OK. It doesn't demand you to put yourself in harm's way again. It's simply just letting go of your right to revenge, your right to hate, and our right to get what's owed to you. Choose forgiveness for each little thing that comes to mind. Bring it to the cross by praying out loud and telling God you forgive that person for what was done just like God forgave you.

God is going to use this book to change your future, so don't let your past hold you back from the victory He has for you every day. What an opportunity Erik and Troy have provided for you to look at 20 essential areas of your life! Take your time with each of them, be honest with what you find, and allow God to walk you through the process to find greater life, peace, freedom and joy in the Green Zone. Godspeed on the journey!

Pastor Karl Leuthauser
Grace Community Church
Montrose, Colorado

PREFACE

I came to a place in my life where I needed something more…more connections, more quality to my life and more quality in my relationships.

I began attending Grace Community Church in Montrose, Colorado with my wife and daughters, and through my connection with Pastor Karl and my new church family, I became a Christian.

As a new Christian I began to understand the excitement and inspiration that a church community can offer. I was most definitely inspired and excited about my connection with my new church family! The message that Pastor Karl delivered, week after week, was without a doubt uplifting, inspirational and motivating!

As I began connecting on a more personal level with my church family, I became aware that many of them seemed to struggle with how to directly apply Pastor Karl's message throughout the week. And, I noticed *I* was struggling with the same challenge.

How do I take this strong connection with God that I feel on Sunday and apply it throughout the week when I am *overwhelmed* by Wednesday!

I wanted to take that special connection and inspiration that I experienced in church and apply it to my relationships. I know the quality of my relationships equals the quality of my words and behaviors. I just needed applicable tools that would specifically help me strengthen the quality of those relationships.

I also recognized that the same challenges that surface in counseling with my clients are also the same challenges that we, as Christians, face on a daily basis. We know that we need to connect with other people in healthy ways to build meaningful and high quality relationships but often times we don't believe we have applicable ways and tools to achieve it.

Troy, my co-author for this book and my brother-in-law, grew up going to church with his family but struggled to hang on to those teachings as he transitioned into adulthood. He tried many things to fill that void. Troy's wife, Jeni, and his children lead him back to the church where he accepted Christ as his Savior in 1994. He, too, was looking for tools in his faith to help strengthen the quality of his relationships.

Troy and I both agreed that we needed applicable, authentic tools that would give us focus and direction as to how to apply God's Word to our daily lives.

We believe that God has given us a clear set of virtues to use as tools to apply His Word to every aspect of our lives. We have chosen twenty of these virtues that we feel are scripturally driven and applicable to our daily lives.

Our mission is to introduce you to a simple set of tools we developed that are relevant and realistic, and educate you on how to use them. These tools will absolutely influence your words, actions and deeds 100% of the time. We believe that when you are using these tools as they were designed to be used, you will experience the peace, contentment and satisfaction that we call *"Walking with God in the Green Zone"*.

Erik S. Cooper, M.A., LMFT
Montrose, Colorado
May, 2016

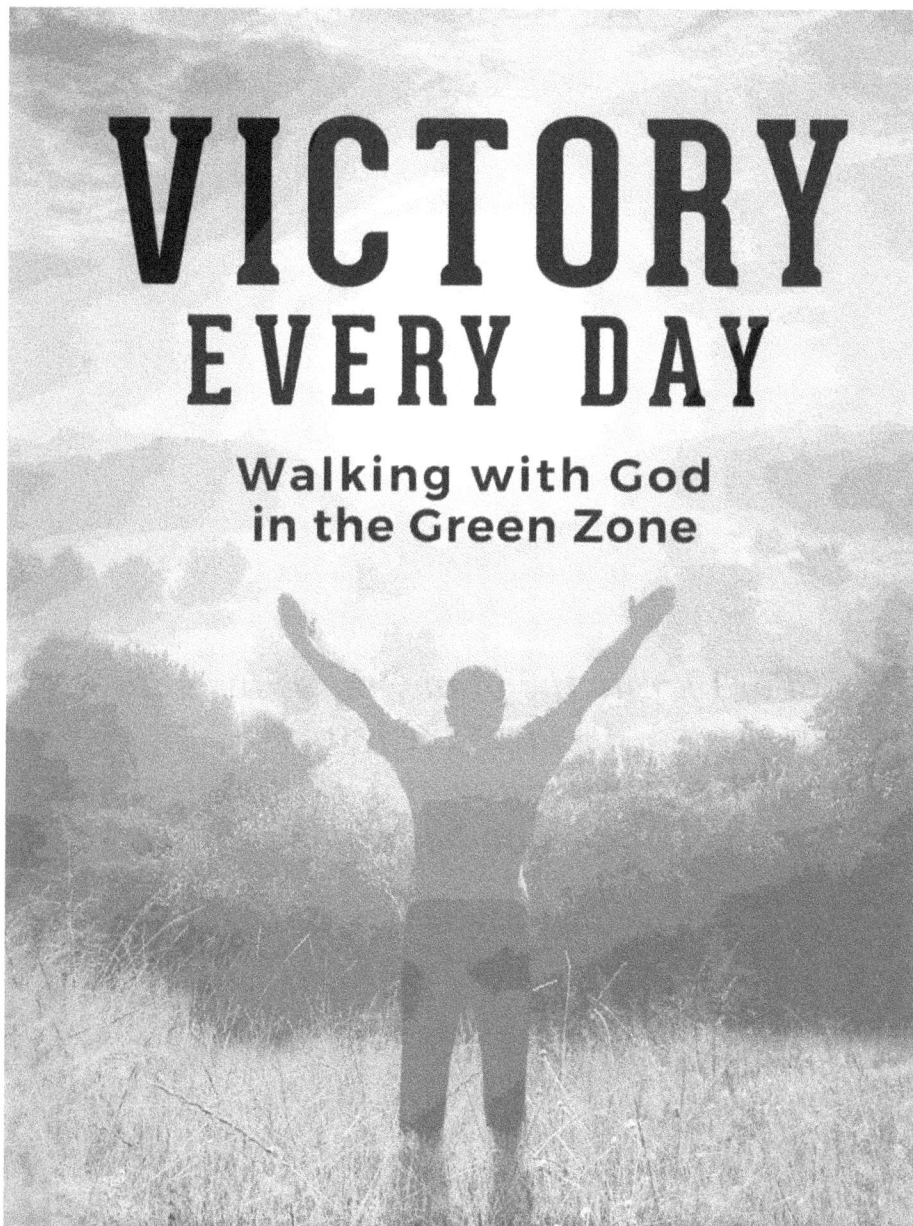

VICTORY EVERY DAY

Walking with God in the Green Zone

"For I know the plans I have for you,"
declares the Lord,
"plans to prosper you and not to harm you,
plans to give you hope and a future."

JEREMIAH 29:11 (NIV)

~ 1 ~
ARE YOU THRIVING OR MERELY SURVIVING IN YOUR DAILY WALK WITH GOD?

All of us know at least one person who goes through life experiencing drama after drama, crisis after crisis. These same folks make their decisions based solely upon their emotions. They tend to put their feelings in the driver's seat of their life experiences. Consequently, they soon discover that their lives are filled with more crisis and chaos than they want or can manage. In order to function, they are forced to think of all the "what ifs" in life because they are operating in a reactive mode which is a very stressful existence. This kind of reactive action is what we call surviving. Just getting by.

However, when we choose not to allow emotions to rule our lives, we are able to operate in a more responsive or proactive manner. In this way, we can achieve more consistency and more predictability in our lives, and it is easier to push through the many day-to-day challenges that are sure to face us.

An important fact of being proactive instead of reactive is that we can operate more from a place of character as part of our inner-being and decision-making process. Being proactive allows us to thrive and not merely survive.

Survival lacks focus and direction. Thriving is a result of having focus and a direction. For example, imagine a man drowning in the middle of the ocean, kicking his legs and waving his arms, exerting a great deal of energy just to stay afloat. We call this just surviving.

Now imagine that same man getting a glimpse of a boat or an island in the distance. He now has a specific focus and direction. That same man is shifting from surviving to thriving. He knows where he is going and how he needs to get there.

SHIFTING YOUR FOCUS

Simply put, we want you to change your focus. You choose where you want to put your focus. We know that what you focus on and where you place your intention, will set the target of what you will reach. If you focus on something that you would rather not have happen, then, that is where your intention will be—on the negative, exactly what you don't want.

JESUS WALKS ON WATER

Immediately Jesus made the disciples get into the boat and go on ahead of him to the other side, while he dismissed the crowd. After he had dismissed them, he went up on a mountainside by himself to pray. Later that night, he was there alone, and the boat was already a considerable distance from land, buffeted by the waves because the wind was against it.

Shortly before dawn Jesus went out to them, walking on the lake. When the disciples saw him walking on the lake, they were terrified. "It's a ghost," they said, and cried out in fear.

But Jesus immediately said to them: "Take courage! It is I. Do not be afraid."
"Lord, if it's you," Peter replied, "tell me to come to you on the water."

"Come," he said.

Then Peter got down out of the boat, walked on the water and came toward Jesus. But when he saw the wind, he was afraid and, beginning to sink, cried out, "Lord, save me!"

Immediately Jesus reached out his hand and caught him. "You of little faith," he said, "why did you doubt?"

And when they climbed into the boat, the wind died down. Then those who were in the boat worshiped him, saying, "Truly you are the Son of God." (Matthew 14:22-33 New International Version)

Peter had to make the choice to either focus on Jesus or focus on his fears and obstacles. When Peter chose to focus on Jesus, he was able to walk on water through the stormy waters towards Jesus. As Peter started losing his focus and direction, he became consumed with the stormy waters. He was focusing on his fears and obstacles and merely surviving. When Peter shifted his focus from Jesus to his fears, he inevitably began to sink. Jesus reminded Peter to remain focused and not doubt his faith. As Jesus reached out his hand, Peter regained his focus and walked to Jesus. Peter took a leap of a faith and experienced the first step to thriving in his relationship with Jesus Christ.

Peter is the only other man in the Bible, besides Jesus, to walk on water. Peter's experience is a profound example for us to focus on Jesus in the midst of life's obstacles. Not because obstacles don't exist, but because we know that regardless of the obstacles or doubts we face in our daily lives, as long as our focus and faith remain on Jesus, we can get through anything.

~ 2 ~

BUILDING A FOUNDATION

Do you want to build a foundation for yourself, your family and all those around you?

Building the foundation of a house begins with laying rebar – connecting metal rods in a checkerboard fashion to support the concrete when it hardens. The rebar is what gives the concrete foundation strength and form. Figuratively speaking, character is the rebar that gives a person a strong foundation in building a meaningful life.

It is not always obvious by looking at the outside of a foundation whether or not it contains rebar. However, when a poorly built foundation experiences an inevitable, unexpected shift, the house built on it weakens creating severe structural damage.

When the foundation for a family is weak, it usually lacks the "rebar" or the "character strengths" to weather life's storms. The old adage, "Murphy's Law", says "anything that can go wrong will go wrong". Life challenges come in clusters. Life tends to toss new challenges at us before we have managed to resolve the present one. Some events are so difficult we feel as if we cannot handle one more crisis! Then, something else happens to further disrupt things, adding more pressure and stress.

When this happens, the "foundation" of the family is either strong enough to withstand crisis or it becomes severely weakened, causing the family structure to crumble. The condition of the foundation is a primary factor.

~ 3 ~

THE TIMELESS TWENTY TOOLKIT©

Using the toolkit from a Christian perspective to build your personal foundation

"Everyone then who hears these words of mine and does them will be like a wise man who built his house on the rock. And the rain fell, and the floods came, and the winds blew and beat on that house, but it did not fall, because it had been founded on the rock. And everyone who hears these words of mine and does not do them will be like a foolish man who built his house on the sand. And the rain fell, and the floods came, and the winds blew and beat against that house, and it fell, and great was the fall of it."(Matthew 7:24-27 NIV)

Do you crave more peace, contentment and satisfaction in your life? Are you ready to learn how to navigate around life's obstacles?

The Timeless Twenty Toolkit© is a set of "character" tools that will help steer you toward healthier relationships and a fulfilling and peaceful life. In this section, we introduce you to 20 time-tested tools that we guarantee will change your perceptions and your life –if you choose to use them consistently.

We invite you to pick up your toolkit and fill it with the most valuable and priceless tools you will ever use to build the life you've always wanted!
We believe that character is the cornerstone to a healthy foundation for ourselves and those around us. As Christians, we believe that God gave us virtues to apply and shape character in ourselves so that we build our lives on the rock and not the sand.

Many of us are looking for a clear path of what God wants us to do. We struggle with the uncertainty of truly knowing that we are living our lives in alignment with our relationship with God. Sometimes we struggle with loneliness, feeling disconnected from others and from life in general – mentally, emotionally, physically and spiritually disengaged from each other.

What are the right decisions? How do we know? What is God's will for us? What would Jesus do? Where can we find the applicable guidance to make healthy decisions as we face these daily challenges?

The good news is that through scripture, God has provided a clear set of virtues to help us find answers to these questions and to be in alignment with His will!

"But the fruit of the Spirit is love, joy, peace, long-suffering, gentleness, goodness, faith, meekness, temperance: against such there is no law." (Galatians 5:22-23 NIV)

These virtues are as important today as they were when Paul spoke to the Galatians about the difference between being saved by faith and being saved by law. Paul explains that faith in Christ is enough to save us from human weakness, and that we can partake of the Fruit of the Spirit, in love, joy, peace, long-suffering, gentleness, goodness, faith, meekness and temperance to lift others up and live in alignment with God's will.

We believe these virtues are actual tools we can use to help build and strengthen our character. Because of this, we will be referring to these virtues as "character tools". We chose twenty of these virtues/character tools because they are timeless and are also the basic building blocks to healthy relationships with everyone in our lives. Thus, the **Timeless Twenty Toolkit**©.

These tools are designed to help you build a strong personal foundation that will enhance the quality of your relationships. The quality of your life is equal to the quality of your relationships. The quality of your relationships is entirely connected to your personal foundation.

These tools are the building blocks for a healthy and fulfilling life. They are essential to building a healthy foundation for all our relationships.

"Victory Every Day: Walking with God in the Green Zone©" is written from a Christian perspective. We have chosen scriptural passages that will enhance your understanding of these tools and how they relate to your daily life.

"Victory Every Day: Walking with God in the Green Zone©" offers people applicable character tools that will create change in the quality of their lives by changing the quality of their relationships. We will show you that there is a direct correlation between using these Timeless Twenty© character tools and living a life of peace, contentment and satisfaction. You will find that you are most connected with God when you are using the Timeless Twenty© character tools!

This is not just a theory but a way of life that has been reinforced by how well Erik's clients have been able to apply the tools to their lives in a way that builds a foundation of strength and stability for them and their families. Erik has used these character tools in a toolkit format to give his clients the opportunity to choose character to build a foundation of stability and inspiration in all their relationships. Over the past years Erik has given hundreds of his clients the Timeless Twenty© character tools to use daily. We have discovered that people who use the Timeless Twenty© character tools consistently improve their relationships, bring stability to their lives and those around them, and create a foundation to weather any of life's challenges.

We believe that it is time to bring character tools back into our daily lives. Utilizing the twenty character tools in the "Timeless Twenty Toolkit© will provide focus and direction, and will ultimately strengthen our relationships leading us to peace, contentment, and satisfaction in our lives.

~ 4 ~

THE CHARACTER TOOL GAUGE

So, how do you know when you're using each tool in the way God intended it to be used?

As you study and learn more about each of the Timeless Twenty© character tools, your awareness and newly learned skills will strengthen as you focus on your connection with God.

We have provided you with a way to assess whether you are truly living in alignment with God. The *Character Tool Gauge©* will help you identify when you are using the tool and in alignment with God or *misusing* the tool and out of alignment with God.

Picture this gauge with a red zone on each end and a green zone in the middle. The red zone to the *left* indicates a "lack of connection with God" and the red zone to the *right* signifies "using your implied connection with God to manipulate others for your own benefit."

The Character Tool Gauge helps you visualize and stay focused on where you want to be... in the Green Zone!

When you are operating in the Green Zone, you are using the Character Tools as they were intended to be used, and you are most connected to God. When we get in the habit of applying these Character Tools to all our relationships, we will find the peace, contentment and satisfaction that we are looking for in our lives. **The green zone is right where God wants you to be!**

~ 5 ~

WALKING WITH GOD
IN THE GREEN ZONE

It's all about focus and direction. The healthiest and strongest application of the character tools requires us to focus on facing forward, forgiveness, and having a Jesus mind-set. These three steps will help you stay focused on Walking with God in the Green Zone© – where, ultimately, you want to be every day.

FACE FORWARD

"Trust in the LORD with all your heart and lean not on your own understanding; in all your ways acknowledge Him, and He will make your paths straight."
(Proverbs 3:5-6 New Living Translation)

"Your word is a lamp to my feet and a light for my path."
(Psalm 119:105 NIV)

"Nevertheless, the righteous will hold to their ways, and those with clean hands will grow stronger."
(Job 17:9 NIV)

Facing forward is the first step to Walking with God in the Green Zone©. Have you ever been successful at winning a race by running backwards? It's impossible! Do you drive your car only focusing on the rear view mirror? You will definitely be able to focus on where you have been but it will be at the cost of you crashing in the present!

When we are facing forward and focused we can be present for anyone or anything. We are most intelligent when we are present. We are the most loving when we are present. We are the best problem solvers when we are present. We are the most compassionate when we are present. We can only connect with God when we are present.

When we are constantly "looking in the rear view mirror", we are focusing on the past and events that cannot be changed. Focusing on the past means we will continue to re-experience the same thoughts, the same emotions and the same perceptions as we relive the experiences that brought us pain and/or regret. When we are consumed with our past, we are likely to be consumed with the pain and suffering associated with the past.

Why focus on something that will never change? When we choose to accept that the past will never change, no matter how long or how many times we look at it, we can then choose to turn around and move forward…. toward the green zone.

FORGIVENESS

"Then Peter came to Jesus and asked, 'Lord, how many times shall I forgive my brother when he sins against me? Up to seven times? 'Jesus answered, 'I tell you, not seven times, but seventy-seven times'". **(Matthew 18: 21-22 NIV)**

We forgive so that we can be in the present with our relationships and with God. If we are not forgiving, then what are we doing?

Living with resentment and living in the past! Be ready to forgive again and again.

Revenge and injustice are the two largest obstacles that stop us from forgiving someone. Forgiveness allows us to "move on" from a bad experience. Choosing not to forgive keeps us focused on the past. Revenge says, "I want you to feel and know how much pain you have caused me and how much you have affected my life". Revenge is a huge obstacle to navigate around.

Injustice says, "I don't think this is fair". Injustice is another mountain to climb on the way to forgiveness. When we feel so angry that we cannot forgive, we want revenge. We are motivated, actually driven, by injustice.

When our thoughts about revenge overwhelm us with thoughts of, "It just isn't fair," it is the injustice that traps us. The reason? We are focusing on the past and not on the present, where we can find balance and peace.

Many people have a very difficult time with forgiveness, often mistaking it for permissiveness, even weakness.

Forgiveness does not necessarily have to be verbalized to the other person. It is just as powerful to express it to yourself.

"I forgive you because I choose to not carry this burden around anymore. The energy it takes from me to focus on the situation is at the cost of me being in the present. Since I cannot be in the past and the present at the same time, I choose the present."

Often this type of forgiveness can be better understood when thinking of it as accepting the situation as it is and then choosing to turn around and face forward.

What's getting in the way of your forgiveness? Perhaps it is the direction of your feet. Turn around, stop focusing on the past and face forward. Choosing not to forgive keeps us tethered to our past.

Forgiveness is our path to the Green Zone.

THE JESUS MIND-SET

Do nothing out of selfish ambition or vain conceit. Rather, in humility value others above yourselves, not looking to your own interests but each of you to the interests of the others. In your relationships with one another, have the same mindset as Christ Jesus. **(Philippians 2:3-5 NIV)**

For even the Son of Man did not come to be served, but to serve, and to give his life as a ransom for many." **(Mark 10:45 NIV)**

Jesus replied, "you must love the lord your god with all your heart, all your soul and all your mind. This is the first and greatest commandment. And the second is equally important: 'love your neighbor as yourself.' the entire law and all the demands of the prophets are based on these two commandments." **(Matthew 22:37-40 NIV)**

We believe that we should have the same mindset as Christ in all of our relationships. In other words, we are here on this earth to serve others and lift them up.

Jesus came to this earth as a servant to man. As a servant, he offered us a gift. His Gift is that He sacrificed his life for us because he knew that because we are of the world, we are sinners. He knew that because we are sinners, our works alone would never allow us enter the Kingdom of Heaven. His crucifixion and sacrificial blood he spilled for us washes away our sins when we accept His Gift. In giving His life for us, He placed our needs ahead of his own!

Jesus also gave us the number one commandment: to love the Lord our God with all our heart, soul and mind. He gave us the second commandment to love our neighbor as ourselves, but said it was equally as important as the number one commandment. If we have the same sacrificial love for others that Jesus has for us we will always have the right perspective going into each relationship.

When we strive to have the same mindset as Christ Jesus, we will always know which character tools to use to lift up others and live in alignment with God's will...Walking with God in the Green Zone©. *Victory Every Day!*

VICTORY EVERY DAY

Victory Every Day means learning and choosing to use theologically sound character tools that are God-driven.

Victory Every Day is the comfort and confidence that comes from knowing with certainty that using these character tools will align and strengthen our relationship with God.

Victory Every Day means that our relationships are healthy and in alignment with God's will.

Victory Every Day means that we are at peace and genuinely content.

E These character tools are essential to our well-being. I believe they are as vital to us as oxygen is to our existence. Using these character tools every day is our way to breathe God into every one of our relationships. I have found that people, by and large, feel very disconnected. They want something different. They may not know what they want, but they know they want to experience peace, contentment and satisfaction in their life each day.

I believe that each day we have a choice as to whether or not we experience the peace, contentment and satisfaction we desire. It comes down to whether we are willing to choose to use these character tools that have a 100% guarantee to strengthen every aspect of our life.

(T) *Victory Every Day* means that I realize the responsibilities that I have to each person in my life, and that I choose to use these God-driven character tools to make their lives better.

As a young man, I looked at responsibility differently than I do today. I tended to see my responsibilities as a burden, rather than as an opportunity to serve. With marriage came the responsibility to be a good husband and provider. When the children were born I had the responsibility to be a good father. It seemed like the older I got, more responsibilities were heaped on my shoulders.

I was consumed with fear that I could not live up to these responsibilities. I was unsure of how to be a good husband, father and provider. I wanted to do it but I just didn't know how. Sometimes, it was so overwhelming that it made me wonder, *"Is this really all there is to life?"*

In the mid 90's, I became a born-again Christian. Although I grew up in the church, I never really accepted Jesus Christ into my life as my Savior. As a new Christian, I started to look at my responsibilities differently.

I realized that Jesus placed more importance on my future well-being than He did on His own life. He was willing to die as a sacrifice for me, a sinner, so I could have eternal life in heaven with God. Jesus was put on this earth to serve mankind, and I believe through his sacrifice for me that I have the opportunity to serve others as well.

As I looked for opportunities to serve the people in my life, I realized that the best way to serve them was to live up to my responsibilities. Meaning that, I should be as good a husband as I can be, be as good a parent as I could possibly be, be a good employee to my boss, and be a good friend to my friends.

I believe that through Scripture, God has given us the character tools and the instructions on how to use them, to help make the lives of those around us better. When I choose to use a character tool to make someone's life better that becomes a victory for me, and a victory for God!

Each day, I approach life knowing that God has given me everything I need to meet my responsibilities. I am no longer afraid of nor do I feel burdened by responsibility. "Responsibility" now means that I have an opportunity to serve others. Living up to these responsibilities each day gives me the greatest peace, contentment and satisfaction that I could ever ask for.

And, most important, when I do not live up to all of my responsibilities I know that God still loves me. I know that tomorrow he will give me another opportunity to use the tools and serve others. It is my choice to strive to live up to these responsibilities each day and to serve others to the best of my ability. Walking with God in the Green Zone is *my* victory every day.

~ 6 ~
HOW TO APPLY THE TOOLS

Initially, people don't always *like* therapy. However, they *do* like the practical step-by-step applicable tools that come out of the therapeutic process.

This is why people develop the concept that the therapeutic process only works in the therapist's office. This creates a very dependent, very limited relationship. This means the only time we can make changes is in the therapist's office. That is a powerless position to be in..."I can't do this without my therapist or pastor".

We created this book as a roadmap to help people make changes through an applicable step-by-step process that has longevity. We have included scripture to inspire and instruct you as to God's directives for the use of these tools. These scripture passages validate God's plan for us.

We suggest reading through the book at least once, and then commit to spending one week on exploring each tool. Each section includes a series of questions to contemplate throughout the week as you implement each tool, and our personal perspectives on using the tools in our own lives. Those paragraphs are marked with our initials "E" (Erik) and "T" (Troy).

In the past 24 years of his practice, Erik has found that there is a direct correlation between using the tools found in the **Timeless Twenty Tool Kit**© and being able to lay your head down on your pillow at the end of the day with peace, contentment and satisfaction. This peace, contentment and satisfaction is a result of knowing that you are doing everything you can to promote healthy relationships with everyone you come into contact with!

Are you ready to walk with God in the Green Zone?

"Give thanks to the Lord, for He is good.
His love endures forever."
PSALM 136:1

"This is the day that the Lord has made;
let us rejoice and be glad in it."
PSALM 118:24

1 GRATITUDE

Gratitude is synonymous with thankfulness and appreciation. It is an attitude and acknowledgment of a benefit that one has received or will receive. Gratitude is not merely feeling grateful, but it is a choice to be motivated by that gratitude to do something outside of yourself.

We believe that feeling and showing gratitude is critically linked to our mental health. Studies show that when we express gratitude, our overall quality of life and well-being benefit significantly. We have found that the best way to begin to acknowledge and show gratitude is by keeping a daily journal listing the things for which we are grateful. A simple way to begin using this tool is to list three things daily that you choose to be grateful for. We are confident that once you start this process, you will notice a positive impact on your attitude, relationships and daily life.

WHY PRACTICE GRATITUDE?

Over the past decade, hundreds of studies have documented the social, physical, and psychological benefits of gratitude. The research suggests these benefits are available to most anyone who practices gratitude, even in the midst of adversity. Here are some of the top research-based reasons for practicing gratitude.

- Gratitude brings us happiness: In research by Robert Emmons, happiness expert, Sonja Lyubomirsky[1], and many other scientists, practicing gratitude has proven to be one of the most reliable methods for increasing happiness and life satisfaction; it also boosts feelings of optimism, joy, pleasure, enthusiasm, and other positive emotions.
- Gratitude reduces anxiety and depression.

---

[1]http://greatergood.berkeley.edu/topic/gratitude/definition-46k-Robert Emmons: Benefits of Gratitude. The Greater Good Science Center/University of California/Berkeley

- Gratitude is good for our bodies: Studies by Emmons and his colleague Michael McCullough suggest gratitude strengthens the immune system, lowers blood pressure, reduces symptoms of illness, and makes us less bothered by aches and pains. It also encourages us to exercise more and take better care of our health.
- Grateful people sleep better: They get more hours of sleep each night, spend less time awake before falling asleep, and feel more refreshed upon awakening. If you want to sleep more soundly, count blessings, not sheep.
- Gratitude makes us more resilient: It has been found to help people recover from traumatic events, including Vietnam War veterans with PTSD.
- Gratitude strengthens relationships: It makes us feel closer and more committed to friends and romantic partners. When partners feel and express gratitude for each other, they each become more satisfied with their relationship. Gratitude may also encourage a more equitable division of labor between partners.
- Gratitude promotes forgiveness.
- Gratitude makes us "pay it forward": Grateful people are more helpful, altruistic, and compassionate.
- Gratitude is good for kids: When 10-19 year olds practice gratitude, they report greater life satisfaction and more positive emotions, and they feel more connected to their community.
- Gratitude is good for schools: Studies suggest it makes students feel better about their school; it also makes teachers feel more satisfied and accomplished, and less emotionally exhausted, possibly reducing teacher burnout.

E *I believe gratitude is looking at my life and knowing that I have enough. Choosing gratitude demands that I am in the moment. Being grateful is my opportunity to get connected with God. I believe our deepest sense of gratitude comes through grace. It is an awareness that we have not earned, nor do we deserve, what we have been given. When people desire a connection with God and those around them, gratitude is the vehicle. When I am grateful, I know I have had nothing to do with the reason for my gratitude. I am grateful I have what I have. Gratitude is a whole paradigm shift. It's the ability to see what I have and to not focus on that which I do not have.*

I like to thank God for each day and all the positive and negative events that happen in it. I believe that everything that happens to me each day is an opportunity for me to learn something that will make me a stronger person. Beginning and ending each day with gratitude is something I have tried to instill in my children.

GAUGING YOUR GRATITUDE
Where do you measure up?

FAR LEFT (RED ZONE): YOU ARE NOT GRATEFUL.

- You are unappreciative.
- You are insatiable, unable to be satisfied.

THE MIDDLE (GREEN ZONE): YOU FOCUS ON HAVING GRATITUDE.

- You are connected and in alignment with God.
- The healthy balance of feeling appreciation and being able to express that appreciation in a genuine way.

FAR RIGHT (RED ZONE): YOU USE GRATITUDE IN AN UNHEALTHY WAY.

- You use gratitude as a means of seeking attention.
- You fake being grateful to gain other people's approval.

CONSIDER THIS!

(E) *You can make personal changes in two ways. You can either let your head lead and your heart will follow or you can let your heart lead and your head will follow. Here is an idea to consider. Let's say you are not genuinely choosing gratitude but act grateful anyway. Would you begin to eventually experience genuine gratitude? Absolutely. Sometimes a little "acting" is in order and we need to "fake it 'til we make it".*

It is evidenced-based that simply focusing on gratitude will lower your blood pressure as well as your heart rate. Research also shows choosing to use gratitude strengthens your immune system. Gratitude has the power to heal, energize and change lives. Knowing this information, why would anyone choose not to use this tool?

(T) *I believe God wants us to reach out to others to show gratitude. When you do, you create an immediate response of kindness back to you. It becomes a circle of love that always begins with you showing gratitude to someone else first.*

IF I WERE GRATEFUL RIGHT NOW (If I was able to notice what I *do* have in my life versus what I *don't* have in my life) I WOULD BE GRATEFUL FOR.....

My *intention* is to choose and apply *gratitude* to all areas of my life.

Today, I want to *take responsibility* for choosing to use the tool, GRATITUDE.

**Here are the ways in which I can *walk in gratitude* with God
in the Green Zone:**

PERSONAL:

FAMILY:

WORK:

SOCIAL:

FAITH:

**I will walk in the Green Zone with God today by choosing to use the tool,
GRATITUDE.**

"Let no corrupting talk come out of your mouths, but only such as is good for building up, as fits the occasion, that it may give grace to those who hear."

EPHESIANS 4:29

*"Rejoice with those who rejoice;
mourn with those who mourn."*

ROMANS 12:15

*"Finally, all of you, live in harmony with one another;
be sympathetic, love as brothers,
be compassionate and humble."*

1 PETER 3:8

② SOCIAL AWARENESS

Having a healthy amount of social awareness is necessary both on a personal and professional level. The competencies associated with being socially aware are:

- **EMPATHY**: understanding the other person's emotions, needs and concerns.
- **SERVICE**: the ability to understand and meet the needs of others.
- **ORGANIZATIONAL AWARENESS**: the ability to understand the politics of working within organizations.

Essentially, awareness of social situations is about carefully considering what people want and planning to communicate with them in a way that is intended to meet that need. Great leaders and public speakers are skilled in this ability and it helps them build support. At its worst, social awareness can be calculating and manipulative. At best, being socially aware is a natural response to people, taking their situation and needs into account as much as possible.

Dr. Alan Zimmerman[2] writes: One young man had to learn that the hard way, as my friend Palani at PAL Vision Associates told me. He told me about a young man who went to apply for a managerial position in a big company. He passed the initial interview, and now he was about to meet the director for his final interview. The director discovered from his resume that the youth's academic achievements were excellent. He asked, "Did you obtain any scholarships in school?" The young man answered "no".

"Was it your father who paid for your school fees?"

"My father passed away when I was one year old. It was my mother who paid for my school fees." he replied.

---

[2] Dr. Alan Zimmermans's Tuesday Tip #675, May 20, 2013   www.drzimmerman.com

"Where did your mother work?" The young man said, "My mother worked as a clothes cleaner."

The director asked the job applicant to show him his hands. The applicant showed his that were smooth and perfect. So, the director asked, "Have you ever helped your mother wash the clothes?"

"Never, my mother always wanted me to study and read more books. Besides, my mother can wash clothes faster than me." said the young man.

The director said, "I have a request. When you go home today, go and clean your mother's hands, and then see me tomorrow morning." The young man felt that his chance of landing the job was high. When he went back home, he asked his mother to let him clean her hands. His mother felt strange, but with mixed feelings, she showed her hands to her son.

The young man cleaned his mother's hands slowly, with tears dripping down his face. It was the first time he noticed that his mother's hands were so wrinkled and so covered in bruises. Some bruises were so painful that his mother winced when he touched them.

This was the first time the young man realized that it was this pair of hands that washed clothes every day to pay for his education. After cleaning his mother's hands, the young man quietly washed all the remaining clothes for his mother. That night, the mother and son talked for a very long time.

The next morning, the young and eager job applicant went to the director's office. The director noticed the tears in the applicant's eyes when he asked, "Can you tell me what you learned at your house yesterday?"

The young man answered, "I cleaned my mother's hands, and I finished cleaning all the remaining clothes. I know now what appreciation is. Without my mother, I would not be who I am today. By helping my mother, I not only realized how difficult it is to get something done on your own, but I also have come to appreciate the importance and value of helping other people."

The director said, "This is what I am looking for in a manager. I want to recruit a person who can appreciate the help of others, a person who knows the sufferings of others to get things done, and a person who would not put money as his only goal in life. You are hired!". The new manager worked very hard and received the respect of his subordinates. Every employee worked diligently and worked as a team. The company's performance improved tremendously. All because this new manager had gained a significant portion of Social Awareness.

As a footnote, let me tell you that a child who is protected and habitually given whatever he wants, develops an "entitlement mentality" and will always put himself first. He would be ignorant of his parent's efforts. When he starts work, he would assume that every person must listen to him, and when he becomes a manager, he would never know the sufferings of his employees and would always blame others when things don't go his way.

A child raised this way may be good academically, and successful for a while, but eventually he would not feel a sense of achievement. He will grumble, be full of hatred, and fight for me-me-me.

You can let your child live in a big house, eat a good meal, learn piano, and watch TV on a big screen. But if you want to raise social awareness in your kids, when you are cutting grass, let them experience it as well. After a meal, let your children wash their plates and bowls together with their brothers and sisters. Let your kids know that even though you could afford a maid, you may not have one...because you want your children to experience the difficulty of learning how to work with others to get things done.

E *Social awareness is a reminder to us that there is more that connects us to each other than separates us. I believe that social awareness reminds us of the value that God wants us to place on our relationships.*

T *I believe that God wants us to connect with people! The best way to begin connecting with people is to start asking questions about things they care about such as their children, their family, and their work. Social awareness begins with genuinely listening and responding to what they say.*

GAUGING YOUR SOCIAL AWARENESS
Where do you measure up?

FAR LEFT (RED ZONE): YOU ARE NOT SOCIALLY AWARE.

- You are self-centered.
- You do not have the ability to "read" others. You lack the ability to understand and interpret what's going on around you.
- You do not step outside of yourself to understand what motivates and drives others.

THE MIDDLE (GREEN ZONE): YOU UNDERSTAND THE EMOTIONS, NEEDS AND CONCERNS OF OTHERS.

- You are connected and in alignment with God.
- You are aware of the motives and feelings of other people.
- You do what is right in order to fit into different situations and with different people.
- You have the ability to put people at ease.
- You have the ability to "read" social cues and to use this information to guide what you do and say.
- You know your limits with different people and show respect for those who hold beliefs that differ from yours.
- You are not contentious, nor do you seek ways to irritate people or see how far you can push others.

- Your social awareness is motivated by self-centered purposes.
- You are able to "read" people but are too much of a "people pleaser."
- You try to please and agree with everyone at the cost of losing your own thoughts, emotions and perceptions.

CONSIDER THIS!

When you choose social awareness, you are respectful and mindful of others. With this tool, you know how to align your actions to meet each social situation so that you are appropriate. This tool reminds us that we are stronger when we join together than we are individually.

I believe God gave us two ears and one mouth for a reason. He wants us to listen twice as much as we speak! Social awareness begins with listening to those around you and then responding to their needs.

**I AM SOCIALLY AWARE WHEN MY FOCUS IS ON THE PEOPLE IN MY LIFE AND HOW I RELATE TO THEM.
THIS ALLOWS ME TO.....**

My *intention* is to choose and apply *social awareness* to all areas of my life.

Today, I want to *take responsibility* for choosing to use the tool,
SOCIAL AWARENESS.

Here are the ways in which I can *walk in awareness* with God in the Green Zone:

PERSONAL:

FAMILY:

WORK:

SOCIAL:

FAITH:

I will walk in the Green Zone with God today by choosing to use the tool,
SOCIAL AWARENESS.

"A cheerful heart is good medicine, but a crushed spirit dries up the bones."
PROVERBS 17:22

"He will yet fill your mouth with laughter and your lips with shouts of joy."
JOB 8:21

3   HUMOR and PLAYFULNESS

Being playful helps you find enjoyment in everyday life. While the modes change, play still helps adults integrate with one another in the same way that it does for children. Playful (and appropriate) behavior can open the mind and soul of human beings to relate more meaningfully to each other. Socially, it can simply be useful as an icebreaker. Being playful in our long-term relationships, like marriages, can often open the doors for intimacy that isn't available otherwise.

It is also important to note how beneficial humor is to us when we are going through difficult times. Laughter is the sudden release of built-up nervous tension and stress. That's why laughter feels so good! Research shows that laughter is very beneficial to our health. Being able to see a particular situation with a sense of humor and playfulness reminds us not to take ourselves too seriously.

Playfulness is connected to the child in us. Do not lose your ability to be playful. Playfulness is not something you outgrow, like clothing. The gauge of when to be playful is dictated by those around you and their comfort level with your playfulness, outgoing style and directness. Being playful is how we connect and bond with one other. Knowing how and when to use humor is a critical skill that feeds life into a relationship.

We want to reemphasize that your humor needs to be healthy and is never at the expense of others. When you choose to use humor in your relationships, make sure that the cues and behaviors of others indicate that your humor is appropriate and acceptable.

Humor is one of the most effective tools to discern the quality of a relationship. When there is laughter, the relationship is healthy. On the other hand, when the laughter stops, the relationship is on the down side. Here are some ways to make sure that laughter remains ever-present.

Humor changes how we feel, how we think, and how we behave. When we feel good, we reach out and connect with others. We are more open to trying new things, taking risks and being open to possibilities. In addition, humor improves our biochemistry! Studies indicate that people who practice humor enjoy an increase in certain antibodies and a reduction in stress hormones, while depressed people experience a suppression of their immune system.

A sense of humor can go a long way toward helping you and your partner get through difficult times. When you lighten up, you take control of your troubles instead of allowing them to control you.

(E) *I'm saddened to see adults so intense and serious that their ability to belly laugh or smile is forgotten. I am aware of how important laughter and playfulness are in my own relationships. I find that being able to play and laugh relieves my stress better than anything else I've come across. Choosing to have humor and playfulness demands that we are present in any particular situation. Being present is significant as it is the only time we can connect with God.*

(T) *Our family, from the youngest to Grandpa, play games such as Monopoly and Yahtze. It brings out the child in us and the whole family has fun. We play games that include everyone so no one feels left out. Games bring out playful energy. Jeni and I bring playful energy to our business meetings. Our customers pick up on how relaxed we are and they relax as well. It helps to solidify our business relationships.*

GAUGING YOUR HUMOR and PLAYFULNESS
Where do you measure up?

FAR LEFT (RED ZONE): YOU HAVE LITTLE OR NO HUMOR.

- You are stern, serious, stuffy, guarded, inhibited, and restrained.
- You are unable to laugh at yourself or see the humor in situations.

THE MIDDLE (GREEN ZONE): YOU APPRECIATE HUMOR.

- You are connected and in alignment with God.
- You are happy, lively, and able to joke with others.
- You are uninhibited; ready to take a few risks.
- You are learning to trust yourself.
- You are pleasant to be with and exhibit an appreciable amount of "spunk." This means that, from your behavior, no one would doubt that you are a lively and fun person to be with.

FAR RIGHT (RED ZONE): TOO MUCH OF A GOOD THING, YOU ARE TOO PLAYFUL.

- You are overly playful, overly humorous; not being serious enough in serious situations.
- You laugh at the expense of others rather than with others.

CONSIDER THIS!

EIn relationships, being playful is an important lesson to connecting with a partner. To get more out of life and "dance well" with others, you need to be able to be humorous and playful. Learn to laugh with yourself and with others. Learn how to stop taking things so seriously that you stop enjoying the moment. And lastly, remember who and what is most important to you...God.

TI have to remind myself to stop taking myself so seriously. When I take myself self too seriously, it clouds my ability to be open to change. Life is about constant change. The more I look at that change with humor and playfulness, the more competent I become at changing!

IF I WERE LOOKING FOR PLACES TO INTEGRATE HUMOR AND PLAYFULNESS IN MY LIFE, I WOULD BEGIN WITH....

My *intention* is to choose and apply *humor and playfulness* to all areas of my life.

Today, I want to *take responsibility* for choosing to use the tool, HUMOR and PLAYFULNESS.

Here are the ways in which I can *walk in humor and playfulness* with God in the Green Zone:

PERSONAL:

FAMILY:

WORK:

SOCIAL:

FAITH:

I will walk in the Green Zone with God today by choosing to use the tool, HUMOR and PLAYFULNESS.

"But those who hope in the Lord will renew their strength. They will soar on wings like eagles; they will run and not grow weary, they will walk and not be faint."
ISAIAH 40:31

"Through whom we have gained access by faith into this grace in which we now stand. And we rejoice in the hope of the glory of God. Not only so, but we also rejoice in our sufferings, because we know that suffering produces perseverance; perseverance, character; and character, hope."
ROMANS 5:2-4

"May the God of hope fill you with all joy and peace as you trust in him, so that you may overflow with hope by the power of the Holy Spirit."
ROMANS 15:13

4 HOPE and OPTIMISM

What is your story? Are you the cookie that crumbles? When something happens to you, when things get difficult and coping with challenges becomes a stretch, are you the person who curls up in a fetal position mumbling, "Call me when it is over." "What am I going to do?" "Why do these things always happen to me?"

It is important to remember that by choosing hope, you are stronger, regardless of the outcome. Hope and optimism is a choice. When you choose to have hope, you also have the belief that a solution is inevitable. Hope is the whisper you hear that tells you, "Keep going. It's going to get better."

There are many different definitions of hope, depending on which theorist you follow. But there are several common themes in all the definitions. Hope usually involves some uncertainty of an outcome, typically concerns matters of importance and usually reflects a person's moral values. Hope is frequently considered a temporary condition that is specific to a given situation. Hope is definitely not the same thing as optimism. It is not the conviction that something will turn out well, but the certainty that something makes sense, regardless of how it turns out.

E *I challenge clients daily regarding their beliefs about their learned helplessness. Many people become so programmed to view themselves as helpless and powerless that they continue to stay imprisoned and tethered to that negative belief structure. Optimism, however, is the belief that future events will have positive outcomes. Optimism has been linked to various aspects of psychological and physical well-being in adults and children. The beneficial effects of optimism and positive coping skills have been shown to enhance one's ability to deal with stress and depression. I believe that optimism is a choice that God gives us in any situation.*

T *I believe that God always wants us to look for the bright side of things. It may be hard to imagine, but I believe there is a bright side to any situation. Choosing optimism can and must be learned. Hope and faith in God is the fuel that keeps you always searching for the bright side.*

GAUGING YOUR HOPE and OPTIMISM
Where do you measure up?

FAR LEFT (RED ZONE): YOU HAVE NO HOPE OR OPTIMISM.

- You are negative, dark, hopeless and desperate.
- You see life as an assembly line, replete with people who have zombie-like movements, all merely going through the motions.

THE MIDDLE (GREEN ZONE): YOU ALWAYS CHOOSE TO LOOK ON THE BRIGHT SIDE.

- You are connected and in alignment with God.
- You have a realistic sense of optimism.
- You look for something positive instead of searching for the negative.
- You start each day excited about the future.
- You are driven by optimism while keeping a hopeful eye on the future.

FAR RIGHT (RED ZONE): YOU HAVE TOO MUCH HOPE OR OPTIMISM.

- You are being rightly criticized for not being real or for being unrealistic. People might accuse you of this behavior by saying, "You always seem to have your head in the clouds."
- You are not prepared for consequences, especially when the future is uncertain.
- You do not combine hope with realism. You may want to be an Olympic contender but you do not have the ability.
- You hope for your wishes to happen, but your energies would be better directed if they were based in realism.

CONSIDER THIS!

E *Our thoughts lead to feelings, which then lead to behaviors. You have a clear choice. You can choose to focus on thinking that things will get better, rather than worrying about all the possible ways that things are going to fail. What you allow yourself to think about or to focus on will absolutely affect how you move through each situation. The difference happens when you choose hope and then let that hope influence your life. Hope is the choice to be open to hearing God telling us through a whisper that it is going to be okay. We have to keep moving forward.*

T *Hope and optimism are like a light that you turn on to make things look even brighter. Shower the people in your life with hope and optimism and pepper your own thoughts with the same. People can pick up on your intentions. It's important to choose to operate with hope and optimism. Having hope means that, whatever you are dealing with, you maintain the belief, "things are going to be okay."*

IF I WERE TO CHOOSE HOPE AND OPTIMISM, MY FOCUS THEN WOULD BE ON.....

My *intention* is to choose and apply *hope* and *optimism* to all areas of my life.

Today, I want to *take responsibility* for choosing to use the tool,
HOPE and OPTIMISM.

Here are the ways in which I can *walk in hope* and *optimism* with God
in the Green Zone:

PERSONAL:

FAMILY:

WORK:

SOCIAL:

FAITH:

I will walk in the Green Zone with God today by choosing to use the tool,
HOPE and OPTIMISM.

"All scripture is God-breathed and is useful for teaching, rebuking, correcting and training in righteousness, so that the servant of God may be thoroughly equipped for every good work."
2 TIMOTHY 3:16

5 SPIRITUALITY

Spirituality is the golden thread of a dynamic web that connects us to God. It unites us to one another and is comprised of the fruits of the Spirit – love, joy, peace, long-suffering, gentleness, goodness, faith, meekness, and temperance that create a common bond for good, and for God.

"But the fruit of the Spirit is love, joy, peace, long-suffering, gentleness, goodness, faith, meekness, temperance, against such there is no law." (Galatian 5:22-23)

The search for meaning in our lives is the process that is richly inspired by our connection with others, ourselves, and most importantly, with God. Spirituality fosters the development and use of our character strengths in all aspects of our life. Spirituality can help us operate from a place of purity, wholesomeness, and authenticity.

Faith is the guidepost that helps us nurture and grow our spirituality. We define faith as having loyalty to God and humankind which, in turn influences our way of living. It is a firm belief or conviction without tangible proof arising from a decision to trust. Faith requires us to focus on God. Faith makes us stronger as individuals.

God calls us to choose to stand for something outside of ourselves by changing our focus to the needs of others versus falling for seduction temptations that focus on what's in it for me. Inspiration from God comes in the form of love, security and acceptance. When you are looking for inspiration, be assured that if it is of God, it will be an uplifting message. "God moments" are not about fear, anxiety or other self-depreciating thoughts, or about being self-absorbed. **When you choose spirituality as an operating tool in your life, you choose to never be alone.**

E *Spirituality is all about relationships. It encompasses my relationship with myself, with others, with my environment and with my God. My spirituality helps me remain centered and more connected in these relationships as my faith in God expands and grows.*

T *For me, Spirituality, is my Christian faith. It is my reminder that there is more in life than just me. My faith is the connection to God that gives me a purpose and a plan for how I live my life each day. Faith gives me the fuel to always focus on the needs of those around me.*

GAUGING YOUR SPIRITUALITY
Where do you measure up?

FAR LEFT (RED ZONE): YOU LACK A SENSE OF SPIRITUALITY, PURPOSE AND FAITH.

- You feel separate and alone.
- You believe that when you die, you are gone. Dead.
- You feel you only have yourself to count on.

THE MIDDLE (GREEN ZONE): YOU HAVE A SENSE OF SPIRITUALITY, PURPOSE AND FAITH.

- You are connected and in alignment with God.
- You show respect, honoring or paying tribute to the idea that there is something greater than you that guides how life unfolds.
- You believe that you should be reaching out to assist the sick, the needy and the less fortunate.
- You know that your faith will bring you peace, joy and happiness.
- You have a sense of a greater being that provides life balance and keeps you centered on your pathway.

FAR RIGHT (RED ZONE): YOU RELY ON FAITH INSTEAD OF TAKING PERSONAL RESPONSIBILITY

- Your faith relieves you of the responsibility of coping with life and taking responsibility for your choices and the situation you are in.
- You are living life by a rigid religious order or cult. You are not practicing logical, common sense or social awareness, nor seeing your surroundings for what they really are.
- You demand or insist that all of your beliefs must be adopted by all, and all must abide by your religious directives or doctrine.
- You expect to be rescued in troubled times. You are not willing to make an effort on your own behalf to save yourself.

CONSIDER THIS!

E *Spirituality is the thread that ties us together as we rise above ourselves searching for meaning in our lives through our relationship with God. Spirituality is focusing on the green zone. It encompasses using all the character tools in alignment with God's desire for us to inspire and lift others up.*

T *My Christian faith is like having a navigational compass that always points me in the right direction as I travel my life path.*

I EXPERIENCE A SENSE OF FAITH WHEN I.....

My *intention* is to choose and apply *faith* to all areas of my life.

Today, I want to *take responsibility* for choosing to use the tool, SPIRITUALITY.

Here are the ways in which I can *walk in faith* with God in the Green Zone:

PERSONAL:

FAMILY:

WORK:

SOCIAL:

FAITH:

I will walk in the Green Zone with God today by choosing to use the tool, SPIRITUALITY.

"For God did not give us a spirit of timidity, but a spirit of power, of love and of self-discipline."
2 TIMOTHY 1:7

"Be strong and courageous. Do not be afraid or terrified because of them, for the LORD your God goes with you; he will never leave you nor forsake you."
DEUTERONOMY 31:6

6 COURAGE

The root of the word courage is "cor" — the Latin word for "heart". In one of its earliest forms, the word courage had a very different definition than it does today. Courage originally meant, "to speak one's mind by telling all one's heart." Over time, this definition has changed. Today, courage is synonymous with being heroic. Heroics are appreciated and we certainly need heroes! Perhaps we've lost touch with the idea that speaking honestly and openly about who we are, about what we're feeling, and about our experiences (positive or negative) can also be a definition of courage.

Courage is not something we are born with or that can be given to us. Courage is a desirable quality that we practice. We believe courage is the ability and willingness to confront whatever it is that prevents us from moving forward. Whether it is fear, pain, danger, uncertainty or intimidation, we use courage as a vehicle to move forward.

We can choose physical courage when we confront physical pain, hardship, death or the threat of death.

We can choose moral courage to stand up for what is right and ethical especially when presented with popular opposition, shame, scandal or discouragement.

The thought of choosing courage can be overwhelming at times. Our intention is to inspire people to look at every given moment to choose to be courageous. The variety of interactions that we have in all our relationships provides us with opportunities to choose courage every day. Making one courageous decision in the midst of fear is courage. We believe that those individual moments of choosing courage will grow exponentially over time and infiltrate all our relationships.

"Courage is not the absence of fear. It is acting in spite of it."~ Mark Twain

E I believe courage is a quality that we can develop and model for our children. We do this when we openly and honestly choose to overcome the fears or obstacles that prevent us from moving forward or taking action. Courage drives our children to tell the truth even when they don't believe it's in their best interests. Courage keeps our children from writing off a friend who has taken a wrong turn in life. Courageous generosity motivates our children to give their allowance to a food bank instead of buying a new video game for their gaming system.

Courage is a huge theme in my life. It seems that I'm either praying for some courage or feeling grateful for having found a little bit of courage to move forward. Likewise, I'm appreciating it in other people. I don't think that makes me unique. Everyone wants to be brave.

T I have experienced many situations which have required me to choose the character tool, courage, in order to move forward. Job changes along my career pathway and other tough decisions all taught me to choose courage in the face of fear. This gave me a chance for new opportunities rather than be stuck in a position I didn't like. Choosing courage in tough situations enabled me to reach for something new. I had enough faith and courage that I was able to apply my skill sets to new situations enabling me to adapt. I believe the sign of a courageous person is someone who feels fear, recognizes fear and still goes on to do what he or she believes is right.

GAUGING YOUR COURAGE
Where do you measure up?

FAR LEFT (RED ZONE): YOU ARE NOT CHOOSING COURAGE.

- Your decisions are solely emotion-based. Making decisions based on fear might be expressed as, "I'm not even going to try for the promotion because I might not get it" or "I'm not going to answer the question because I might be wrong and people will think I'm stupid."
- You fear rejection. Fear of rejection might sound like, "I won't ask so-and-so out on a date because she might not see me as being good enough" or "I am fearful to stand up for what is right because others might reject me."
- You allow your fear to paralyze you preventing you from making any decisions.
- You allow the negative "what ifs" to dominate your thoughts.

THE MIDDLE (GREEN ZONE): YOU CHOOSE COURAGE IN THE FACE OF FEAR.

- You are connected and in alignment with God.
- You do the right thing in spite of feeling fear.
- You stand up for what is right and ethical.
- You feel fear yet choose to act.
- You persevere in the face of adversity.

FAR RIGHT (RED ZONE): YOU USE COURAGE IN AN UNHEALTHY WAY.

- You do not use the element of fear when making decisions. Example: leaping into a dangerous situation without considering the consequences.
- You act courageous as a means of impressing someone.
- Example: "I'm going to walk the ledge of this building so everyone will think I'm courageous."
- You create crisis and chaos so you can play the role of the hero.

CONSIDER THIS!

E *It is my experience that people who choose to be courageous never regret their decision. People who choose to be motivated solely by fear always end up regretting their choice.*

T *Our faith in God gives us the confidence to choose courage in the face of difficult situations. It is important to not let the what-ifs and potential problems dampen our desire to be courageous.*

IF I WERE TO CHOOSE TO BE COURAGEOUS TODAY, I WOULD.....

My *intention* is to choose and apply *courage* to all areas of my life.

Today, I want to *take responsibility* for choosing to use the tool, COURAGE.

Here are the ways in which I can *walk courageously* with God
in the Green Zone:

PERSONAL:

FAMILY:

WORK:

SOCIAL:

FAITH:

I will walk in the Green Zone with God today by choosing to use the tool,
COURAGE.

"Get rid of all bitterness, rage and anger, brawling and slander, along with every form of malice. Be kind and compassionate to one another, forgiving each other, just as in Christ God forgave you."
EPHESIANS 4:31-32

"But I tell you who hear me: Love your enemies, do good to those who hate you, bless those who curse you, pray for those who mistreat you. If someone strikes you on one cheek, turn to him the other also. If someone takes your cloak, do not stop him from taking your tunic. Give to everyone who asks you, and if anyone takes what belongs to you, do not demand it back. Do to others as you would have them do to you."
LUKE 6:27-36

"Then Peter came to Jesus and asked, 'Lord, how many times shall I forgive my brother when he sins against me? Up to seven times?' Jesus answered, 'I tell you, not seven times but seventy-seven times."
MATTHEW 18:21-22

7 FORGIVENESS and MERCY

Forgiveness makes us stronger because we are essentially accepting something that we cannot change. We are mindfully choosing to be present versus focusing on the past.

Injustice and revenge are the two major reasons for not forgiving. When you think about things in your life where forgiveness was not possible, do you feel that life was not fair to you?

When injustice and revenge have been your focus, you might have wanted to "get even" or show the other person how hurt you were. At times, you may obsess over wanting revenge even though that desire to get even keeps you stuck and unable to move on in life. "I will move forward when you know how hurt I am."

Forgiveness is not forgetting. Forgiveness does not excuse someone for doing something unhealthy nor does it erase an unhealthy event or even validate it. When you forgive, it doesn't mean that you approve of what happened. Forgiveness is simply accepting and choosing not to focus on the past or getting even.

Forgiveness is what you do for yourself – what you give to you, not to other people. It means that you're giving yourself permission to move on with your life. Forgiveness allows you to move forward from a negative event, person or space in time. You can move forward in life and stop driving your car focusing on your rear view mirror. Face forward not backwards!

Forgiveness is a choice. Don't wait for it to suddenly wash over you.

Don't give away your power. The pain of what happened is inevitable, but continuing to suffer is optional. The only person you can control is you. By constantly reliving the pain of what happened, you give away your power to the person who wronged you.

Don't cling to negative feelings. Anger is often an outward sign of hurt, fear, guilt, grief or frustration. While the pain may never completely disappear, forgiveness can help you release the anger and bring those in your life closer to you.

There is no right timeline for forgiveness. For some people, making peace happens suddenly and spontaneously. For others, it takes time and a great deal of thought and effort. You may have to make a conscious effort every day to forgive, and actually say, "I'm letting this go. I'm not going to invest hatred, bitterness, anger, resentment in this person anymore. I am choosing to focus on what is in my life today." You can find closure in forgiveness.

You can't change the things that happened in your life, but you can decide how you interpret and respond to them.

E *Forgiveness reminds me to be present with regard to my relationships. It is a reminder that choices that have been made in the past are not more valuable or more significant than the choices being made today. In the present we are smarter, we are more loving, we are more supportive and we are more connected with God.*

T *I believe that revenge and injustice are the main culprits that keep us from moving forward. When I focus on the past, it prevents me from connecting with God and experiencing the love and joy that I hold in my heart.*

GAUGING YOUR FORGIVENESS and MERCY
Where do you measure up?

- You are condemning.
- You are resentful.
- You are judgmental.
- You are vindictive.

THE MIDDLE (GREEN ZONE): YOU MAKE THE CHOICE TO FORGIVE.

- You are connected and in alignment with God.
- You choose to show mercy.
- You see yourself as accountable and responsible. When you see yourself in this light, you won't blame others for the way you are or for where you are in life.
- You do not cling to negative feelings.

FAR RIGHT (RED ZONE): YOU CHOOSE TO FORGIVE AT THE EXPENSE OF YOUR WELL-BEING.

- Your forgiveness is at the cost of your own self-respect and self-advocacy.
- You find yourself remaining in unhealthy situations and relationships.
- You use forgiveness as a way of surviving and going on to your next unhealthy experience.

CONSIDER THIS!

EI am certain that we have all been both wronged and forgiven. The question is, will we forgive? Can we choose to be courageous in our forgiveness even if the other person doesn't know or doesn't do anything to merit our forgiveness? What choice will you make when the opportunity to forgive comes up again?

TForgiveness is not natural. It is a conscious decision to choose an uncommon reaction. It requires courage to choose to forgive someone. Many people believe that revenge and injustice require courage. I want you to know that an "eye for an eye" philosophy leaves everyone blind.

WHO IS THE MOST DIFFICULT PERSON IN MY LIFE FOR ME TO FORGIVE? WHO HAS THE MOST DIFFICULT TIME FORGIVING ME?

My *intention* is to choose and apply forgiveness and humility
to all areas of my life.

Today, I want to *take responsibility* for choosing to use the tool,
FORGIVENESS and HUMILITY.

Here are the ways in which I can *walk in forgiveness and humility* with God
in the Green Zone:

PERSONAL:

FAMILY:

WORK:

SOCIAL:

FAITH:

I will walk in the Green Zone with God today by choosing to use the tool,
FORGIVENESS and HUMILITY.

"The heart of the discerning acquires knowledge; the ears of the wise seek it out."
PROVERBS 18:15

"It is not good to have zeal without knowledge, nor to be hasty and miss the way."
PROVERBS 19:2

"A simple man believes anything, but a prudent man gives thought to his steps."
PROVERBS 14:15

8 CRITICAL THINKING and OPEN-MINDEDNESS

Critical thinkers are both skeptical and open-minded. They value fair mindedness and respect evidence. Critical thinkers are driven by reasoning. They will look at different points of view and change position when reason leads them to do so. Critical thinkers choose to look at choices and compare those choices to arrive at a solution. Critical thinking is the opposite of "knee jerk" reactions.

Critical thinkers slow down their decision-making process thus minimizing the potential of impulsivity or a lack of objectivity. Critical thinkers will assess the reasons for and against doing something and then make their decision based on the basis of that fair assessment.

Critical thinkers are open-minded even with people they disagree with. They give them a fair hearing because their goal is the truth or the best action. A critical thinker's goal is not simply to confirm what they already believe.

Open-mindedness is the environment that you create that allows you to look at all the scenarios from a healthy point of view. Open-mindedness is the willingness to search actively for evidence against one's favored beliefs, plans or goals, and to weigh such evidence fairly when it is available.

E *Critical thinking and open mindedness are imperative in our lives. I often tell my clients the story of going to the eye doctor for an eye exam. I start the exam by telling the doctor that I believe I don't need glasses...that I see everything there is to see. I was hopeful that the eye test would prove me right. The doctor performed the eye test and then asked me where I wanted to purchase the glasses that I needed. I had convinced myself I saw everything but when I looked at the world through my new lenses, I saw all that I was missing. When I did not wear glasses, my brain made up for the deficit by creating a belief that I was seeing everything...even though I clearly was not. The brain is so efficient that it makes up for what is missing and convinces you that you see everything there is to see, even though you are missing a part of the* *picture. When are you choosing not to wear your glasses in your life? In other words, what is it that is difficult for you to look at in your relationships?*

T *I believe that applied critical thinking is essential for effective planning and problem-solving skills. Critical thinking means my own personal bias will be less influential in my decision-making process.*

GAUGING YOUR CRITICAL THINKING
and OPEN-MINDEDNESS
Where do you measure up?

FAR LEFT (RED ZONE): YOU CHOOSE NOT TO USE CRITICAL THINKING.

- You make decisions based solely on emotions which are inconsistent and unpredictable. This creates crisis and chaos.
- You make impulsive decisions motivated by guilt, shame and or fear.
- You think your way is the only way.

THE MIDDLE (GREEN ZONE): YOU HAVE A CONSISTENT PROCESS TO RELY ON FOR MAKING DECISIONS.

- You are connected and in alignment with God.
- You ask questions.
- You define the problem.
- You examine evidence.
- You analyze assumptions.
- You avoid oversimplification.
- You consider other interpretations.
- You rely on reason rather than on emotion.

- You are fearful of taking risks or making changes.
- You look at all the options but are fearful of taking action.
- Your analysis becomes the end-result, not the means to an end.

CONSIDER THIS!

E *Critical thinking is an intellectual tool that you choose to use when you are in a situation where you need to be mindful and thoughtful about the solutions you are generating. It is a tool designed to help you with your problem-solving skills.*

T *Prepare a plan of action to tackle the challenge in front of you. Be ready with alternatives in case the first plan goes awry. When backed with proper planning and preparation, execution is a simple, straightforward process. Applied critical thinking skills are essential for all effective planning, problem-solving, and decision-making processes. Continuous practice improves your thinking speed and gives you the ability to think on your feet. The ultimate challenge is to train your brain to go beyond natural instinct to arrive at logical conclusions even when making instant decisions.*

WHAT SITUATION IN MY LIFE RIGHT NOW REQUIRES CRITICAL THINKING?

My *intention* is to choose and apply *critical thinking* and *open-mindedness* to all areas of my life.

Today, I want to *take responsibility* for choosing to use the tool, CRITICAL THINKING and OPEN-MINDEDNESS.

Here are the ways in which I can use the tool, CRITICAL THINKING and OPEN-MINDEDNESS, as I *walk* with God in the Green Zone:

PERSONAL:

FAMILY:

WORK:

SOCIAL:

FAITH:

I will walk in the Green Zone with God today by choosing to use the tool, CRITICAL THINKING and OPEN-MINDEDNESS.

"Do not let any unwholesome talk come out of your mouths, but only what is helpful for building others up according to their needs, that it may benefit those who listen."
EPHESIANS 4:29

"Do nothing out of selfish ambition or vain conceit, but in humility consider others better than yourselves."
PHILIPPIANS 2:3

"Therefore encourage one another and build each other up, just as in fact you are doing."
1 THESSALONIANS 5:11

9 RELATIONSHIP AWARENESS
INFLUENCING and INSPIRING OTHERS

The quality of our life is equal to the quality of our relationships. We can improve the quality of our relationships by raising our awareness of the significance of those relationships. Our attentiveness allows us to be thoughtful and mindful to the degree we invest in those relationships. What we shine light on is what grows. The more aware we are of our relationships, the more those relationships strengthen and grow.

It is important to recognize that we do influence and hopefully, inspire others in our relationships. We influence people either in a positive or a negative way. One way to imagine how our influence can positively affect others is to see it as a bubbling spring that flows from us to others and beyond. When we do influence others in a positive way, this spring becomes a river of inspiration that is a positive force that will motivate people and lift them up. This speaks to the analogy that a high tide lifts all boats. The privilege of quietly watching our influence lift others up is one of the greatest rewards of inspiring others.

People, places and experiences that provide positive influence help us move closer to our desired goals. The result is that we can be better than we were yesterday. Can you recall a time when a positive change in your thinking was inspired by someone else that empowered you to move beyond what you initially anticipated?

Jim Rohn[3], author and business philosopher said, "We become the combined average of the five people we hang around most." The higher the concentration of time spent around quality people and similar elements, the higher the quality of output we will have to flow from ourselves to others. We can search out and surround ourselves with people who have already been where we want to go. We can be in places and engage in activities that keep us stretched slightly beyond our comfort zone with the understanding that stretching induces growth. And, we can contribute to the success of others by modeling a positive lifestyle.

---

[3] www.jimrohn.com/resource-library.html.

Life is a continual flow of learning and teaching, inputs and outputs. By being aware of the positive and negative elements in our environments, we will not only incorporate things into our lives that create better results, but we will also have a greater level of vision, belief, and expertise.

Try this formula for influencing and inspiring others:

Challenge + Encourage + Motivate = INSPIRATION

CHALLENGE: Create a demand to be, do and have greater than what presently exists.

ENCOURAGE: Provide an external *"You can do this!"* in a way that it becomes the recipient's permanent internal *"I can do this!"*

MOTIVATE: Instill a sense of purpose that becomes an impetus for achievement.

E *As a therapist, I am always conscious of the power of influence. I have learned that it is not a question of "if" we influence others; it is a question of "how." The destruction that results from negatively influencing the people and relationships around us is devastating. I have seen the detrimental consequences ripple through generations. It often becomes a legacy in a family system.*

And so, I am very aware of the power of my influence during a therapy session with a client. It is critical for my clients as well as all my relationships that I try to motivate people in a positive way. Inspiring others with genuine encouragement allows me to connect with people on a spiritual level and it is always positive. It always lifts people up...including me!

T *I know that my words and actions influence and impact others, either in a positive or a negative manner. I need to be mindful and thoughtful about the messages I am sending and how I am impacting the people around me. If I am negative or pessimistic about a situation, others will sense what I feel. Thus, my emotions might be as contagious as a bad cold.*

GAUGING YOUR RELATIONSHIP AWARENESS
Where do you measure up?

> **FAR LEFT (RED ZONE): YOU ARE NOT AWARE OF AND DO NOT FOCUS ON YOUR RELATIONSHIPS.**

- You are negatively influencing others.
- You are not aware of or sensitive to how your words and actions are affecting those around you.

> **THE MIDDLE (GREEN ZONE): YOU RECOGNIZE AND EXERCISE YOUR ABILITY TO INFLUENCE YOUR RELATIONSHIPS IN A POSITIVE MANNER.**

- You are connected and in alignment with God.
- You are very diligent in making sure that you are investing daily in your relationships in a positive manner.
- You are motivated to influence others in an inspirational way and your words and actions support this.

> **FAR RIGHT (RED ZONE): YOU ARE USING YOUR INFLUENCE AND AWARENESS OF YOUR RELATIONSHIPS TO IMPACT PEOPLE.**

- You influence people to echo your thoughts, emotions and perceptions.
- You use influence to manipulate people to get what you want.
- You lift yourself up at the expense of others.

CONSIDER THIS!

E *Healthy communication is the vehicle to inspire others. You can't influence or inspire unless you can effectively communicate what your vision or goal is and how you plan to achieve it. Inspiration dances with trust. Trust only comes when others share their views with you and believe that you respect their ideas. You must listen as well as speak. Healthy communication is key to strengthening your relationship awareness. Relationship awareness is directly linked with the satisfaction and peace that you desire to feel at the end of the day. The more you invest in your relationships in a positive way, the better the quality of your relationships will be. If you are not investing in your relationships, what are you investing in?*

T *You are going to have an impact on people. It is not a question of "if" you are going to have an impact on them, it is a question of "how" you are going to influence them. The more character tools that you learn and apply to your relationships and your life, the more confidence you will have that you are influencing people in a positive way.*

HOW CAN I USE MY INFLUENCE IN A POSITIVE MANNER TO INSPIRE THE PEOPLE IN MY RELATIONSHIPS?

My *intention* is to choose and apply awareness to all areas of my life.

Today, I want to *take responsibility* for choosing to use the tool,
RELATIONSHIP AWARENESS.

Here are the ways in which I can *walk in awareness* with God
in the Green Zone:

PERSONAL:

FAMILY:

WORK:

SOCIAL:

FAITH:

I will walk in the Green Zone with God today by choosing to use the tool,
RELATIONSHIP AWARENESS.

"Finally, brothers, whatever is true, whatever is noble, whatever is right, whatever is pure, whatever is lovely, whatever is admirable – if anything is excellent or praiseworthy – think about such things."

PHILIPPIANS 4:8

"But as you excel in everything – in faith, in speech, in knowledge, in complete earnestness, and in your love for us – see that you also excel in this grace of giving."

2 CORINTHIANS 8:7

"Jesus replied: 'Love the Lord your God with all your heart, and with all your soul, and with all your mind.' This is the first and greatest commandment."

MATTHEW 22:37-38

⑩ STRIVING FOR EXCELLENCE

Striving for excellence is the attitude and/or process of choosing to do your best at everything you do. Striving for excellence is about knowing yourself and your strengths. It is about realizing and accepting responsibility for the roles and influences that you have on the lives of those around you. This encompasses all your relationships –family, business, social and community.

Many people confuse striving for excellence with striving for perfection. Striving to be perfect is a method of sabotaging our success. Being perfect has no finish line and is unachievable. Striving for excellence is the key to living a super-charged life. Striving implies that we must keep practicing, keep at it and not give up despite failed attempts.

If you want to get the most out of life in every way, then you have to put the most into it. It sounds like a cliché but it is absolutely true – you get out of life what you put into it. We have to put our best foot forward in every endeavor.

When you choose to strive for excellence, you surround yourself with passionate people. You build a network of passionate positive people and frequently spend time with them. People of like minds inspire and support each other. When you choose to strive for excellence, you pour your heart and mind into your activities. You are open to new ideas and adopt an attitude to continually seek ideas for self-improvement. You ask yourself at the end of the day, "Did I give the very best of myself to those around me?"

E *"The quality of a person's life is in direct proportion to their commitment to excellence, regardless of their chosen field of endeavor." This quote by the famous football coach, Vince Lombardi, reminds me that anyone, regardless of their chosen profession or job, can improve the quality of their life with a commitment to excellence.I can choose this attitude anytime and it is not connected to any particular outcome. Each time I choose to use this tool, I directly impact my relationships and my life in a positive way.*

If you're not growing, you're dying. If you're not working for good, you're working for bad. I think of these choices every day as I remind myself of my responsibilities to the people around me. I have found that striving for excellence in all areas of my life is the fuel that drives me to be the best I can be. I know that my measuring stick is that I try to do everything a little bit better today than I did yesterday. Why would I want to do anything else? My family, friends and customers expect and deserve nothing less.

GAUGING YOUR STRIVE FOR EXCELLENCE
Where do you measure up?

FAR LEFT (RED ZONE): YOU CHOOSE NOT TO STRIVE FOR EXCELLENCE IN ANY PART OF YOUR LIFE.

- You are fearful of change.
- You are content to not improve your performance or relationships.
- Your focus is on the obstacles, difficulties and problems of the task at hand.
- You give up in the face of obstacles and present yourself as having no responsibility in the outcome.

THE MIDDLE (GREEN ZONE): YOU CHOOSE TO STRIVE FOR EXCELLENCE IN ALL PARTS OF YOUR LIFE.

- You are connected and in alignment with God.
- You make an agreement with yourself to do the best you can in all areas of your life.
- You establish goals to push you beyond what you believe you are capable of doing.

- Your drive for excellence is at the cost of other areas in your life... most especially your relationships.
- You strive for financial goals that come at the expense of shortchanging your relationships.
- Your drive in one area can leave you lacking in other life areas. For example, I am striving to be a great golfer and it comes at the expense of my job and my relationships.

CONSIDER THIS!

E *Striving for excellence implies that we must keep practicing and not give up despite failed attempts. I believe we must strive for excellence – doing all things in the best possible manner. We do not tolerate or accept second grade, shoddy work in others; hence, we too must be putting our best into the job at hand. Enjoy the work, be enthusiastic with the results, and cheer the people who do excellent work! Conversely, we do not strive for perfection, because it is an impossible state to achieve! In trying to do so, we may become tyrannical, shouting and screaming orders, pushing people to extremes, and become a very unattractive person. Perfection kills the joy of doing any work. Hence, "Strive for excellence, not perfection!"*

T *I do believe that we reap what we sow. Therefore if I want to get the most out of life, I need to put the most into it!*

IF I WERE TO CHOOSE TO STRIVE FOR EXCELLENCE IN ONE AREA OR IN ONE RELATIONSHIP IN MY LIFE, IT WOULD BE.....

My *intention* is to choose and apply excellence to all areas of my life.

Today, I want to *take responsibility* for choosing to use the tool, EXCELLENCE.

Here are the ways in which I can *walk in excellence* with God
in the Green Zone:

PERSONAL:

FAMILY:

WORK:

SOCIAL:

FAITH:

I will walk in the Green Zone with God today by choosing to use the tool,
EXCELLENCE.

"He who guards his mouth and his tongue, guards himself from calamity."
PROVERBS 21:23

"My dear brothers, take note of this: Everyone should be quick to listen, slow to speak and slow to become angry, for man's anger does not bring about the righteous life that God desires."
JAMES 1:19-20

"Like a city whose walls are broken down is a man who lacks self-control."
PROVERBS 25:28

11 SELF-CONTROL

SELF-REGULATION and SELF-MANAGEMENT

Self-control separates us from our ancient ancestors and the rest of the animal kingdom, thanks to our large prefrontal cortices. Rather than respond to immediate impulses, we can plan and evaluate alternative actions and refrain from doing things we will regret. We can also take advantage of these innately human abilities by developing wisdom and willpower.

The importance of developing self-control during our preschool age years is illustrated by a classic longitudinal study conducted at Stanford University in the 1960's by Michael Mischel. The researcher presented two options to hungry four-year-old children. They could have one marshmallow right away or get two marshmallows fifteen minutes later when the researcher returned after running an errand. One third of the children opted for one marshmallow. Years later, a follow-up study was administered when the same participants graduated from high school. Mischel found that the children who waited (for the second marshmallow) now possessed the habits of successful people (Beachman, 2009). They were positive, self-motivated, and persistent in their pursuit of goals (Beachman, 2009). These habits point to successful marriages, higher incomes, and better health. The study also showed that the participants who did not wait earned lower SAT scores, were indecisive, less confident, and stubborn; all predictors of unstable marriages, low incomes, and poor health (Beachman, 2009).

A similar and more recent longitudinal study showed that preschoolers who exhibited high levels of delay-of-gratification, later displayed greater cognitive control than teens who had exhibited lower levels of delay-of-gratification during preschool (Eigsti, Zayas, Mischel, Shoda, Ayduk, Dadlani, Davidson, Aber, and Casey, 2006). Self-control develops when children begin to differentiate between short-term and long-term outcomes. When they realize that a long-term outcome is greater, they choose to delay gratification in their best interest. Researchers have found that the ability to choose delayed rewards increases with age and levels off in the early 30's. The capacity to choose a future reward is a function of the prefrontal lobes of the brain. Such capacity demands, "a special kind of memory in which information about the past and the future can be held in mind, while carrying out the responses needed to accomplish the goal" (Barkley, 2007, p. 52).

Self-management begins with self-awareness. Self-awareness speaks to our ability to be aware of what we are thinking and feeling. Once we become aware of what we are thinking and feeling, we can choose how to manage those thoughts and feelings in a mindful, appropriate and healthy manner. The idea here is to either choose to manage our thoughts and feelings or we choose to allow our thoughts and feelings to manage us.

Familiarizing yourself with your thoughts, emotions, what influences you and how things impact you, allows you to strengthen your self-management and self-control.

When you know yourself better, you're inclined to be a better decision maker. You will be better at making decisions as you know how those decisions will affect you and those around you.

This tool may be more valuable to you than relying solely on your intellect. Becoming aware of what you are thinking and feeling and then choosing what you want to do with those thoughts and feelings can be an essential asset to you. Your self-awareness and self-management skills allow you to connect and interact with people in an authentic and genuine way. When you are aware of what you are thinking and feeling you are less driven by your thoughts and feelings.

This allows you to be present in your interactions with people by focusing on the other person and becoming aware of their needs and feelings, rather than focusing only on what you are thinking and feeling.

E *I believe that when we practice self-control, self-regulation and self-management, we are mindfully and thoughtfully choosing what to focus on. The words and actions we choose speak to our focus and direction. I believe we need to slow down, be responsible, mindful and thoughtful about how our words and actions affect others and impact our relationships. Our words and actions do have tremendous power.*

Before I act, I pray for God to show me how my words and actions will affect those around me. This allows me to see the potential positive and/or negative consequences that may play out because of my actions and/or words. I am convinced that this is a good filter to run everything through before speaking or acting.

GAUGING YOUR SELF-CONTROL
Where do you measure up?

FAR LEFT (RED ZONE): YOU LACK SELF-CONTROL.

- You say whatever comes into your head without consideration or respect for others.
- You do what you want simply because it is what you want.
- You are impulsive. You lack an emotional filter which prevents you from saying certain things out loud.
- You have little self-control over your behavior. You blame others for your negative behavior using it as an excuse for not taking responsibility for your own actions.

THE MIDDLE (GREEN ZONE): YOU OPERATE FROM THE "SWEET SPOT" – THE BALANCE BETWEEN SELF-MANAGEMENT AND SELF-REGULATION.

- You are connected and in alignment with God.
- You are thoughtful about what you do.
- You weigh the consequences of all your actions.
- You have control over your decisions so you know they are appropriate and healthy.
- You know that you are 100% responsible for what you say and do.
- You are appropriately spontaneous.

- You fear making decisions. Thus, decisions are not made.
- You are driven by such rigid self-control that you cannot allow yourself to be playful, fun and vulnerable.
- You have no spontaneity.

CONSIDER THIS!

E *Self-management speaks to your ability to think and feel. It allows you to take a deep breath or a pause to decide if you need to act on every thought and feeling that is going through your head. It is your ability in the midst of conflict with your spouse, your children or your colleagues to choose whether you want to "be right" or to "be happy" in that particular situation.*

This tool activates a process within you that encompasses more than self-management. This process allows you to separate your thoughts and feelings from who you authentically are. Self-management means that you get to manage yourself instead of being managed by the environment or things outside of yourself.

T *I believe that God gives us many opportunities each day to use the tool, "Self-control, Self-regulation and Self-management". By choosing to use this tool you will avoid crises and chaos as your choices will be more consistent and predictable.*

I WOULD BENEFIT FROM CHOOSING MORE SELF-CONTROL, SELF-REGULATION AND SELF-MANAGEMENT IN THESE AREAS OF MY LIFE.....

My *intention* is to choose and apply *self-control* to all areas of my life.

Today, I want to *take responsibility* for choosing to use the tool, SELF-CONTROL.

Here are the ways in which I can *walk with self-control* with God
in the Green Zone:

PERSONAL:

FAMILY:

WORK:

SOCIAL:

FAITH:

I will walk in the Green Zone with God today by choosing to use the tool,
SELF-CONTROL.

"Whatever your hand finds to do, do it with all your might, for in the grave where you are going, there is neither working nor planning nor knowledge nor wisdom."

ECCLESIASTES 9:10

12 ZEST, ENTHUSIAM and ENERGY

Zest is defined as having a sense of enthusiasm, energy, excitement and liveliness. When you lend your enthusiasm or energy to others and then spice it up with zest, you give "life" to relationships. In essence, you give "life" to whatever you do, and you'll feel more alive in the process.

You can rise from bed in the morning like a zombie, unconscious but going through the motions to grab your cup of coffee, or you can start the day with a conscious choice for zest that sets the tone for the rest of your day. You can decide to give 100% of your attention to your family by focusing on them and not yourself. Imagine how everyone might feel if you and your family began their day with a positive outlook! Which appeals to you more?

We believe that choosing zest means living your life with a sense of excitement and energy, and anticipation for the future. It is seeing life as an adventure in which you are an active participant.

When you have zest, you exude excitement and energy while approaching tasks in life. It is important to perform all of your tasks wholeheartedly while also being adventurous, vivacious and energetic.

The character tools Zest and Courage (Tool # 6) go hand in hand. Each fuels the other when completing challenging situations and tasks.

People with zest simply enjoy things more.

Zest is a positive attitude that reflects a person's approach to life with anticipation, energy, enthusiasm and excitement.

E *I believe that when I choose zest it is absolutely contagious. My enthusiasm and energy are contagious in my relationships with my daughters, my wife, my neighbors, my clients, my family and friends. If I am going to give somebody something, why not give them something to lift them up...zest!*

T *I associate zest with my intention to give 100% of my enthusiasm and energy to everything I do. I believe that this rule offers the premise that whatever I do at work or at home, I promise myself to always strive for 100% performance. If I give any less than that, I am shortchanging everyone, including myself. I don't want to do that.*

GAUGING YOUR ZEST, ENTHUSIASM and ENERGY
Where do you measure up?

FAR LEFT (RED ZONE): YOU LACK ZEST, ENTHUSIASM AND ENERGY.

- You are always feeling tired.
- You feel a debilitating sadness.
- You have a pessimistic attitude.
- You are low on energy.
- You are ineffective with others.
- You are unlikely to push yourself.

THE MIDDLE (GREEN ZONE): YOU ARE MOTIVATED WITH ZEST, ENTHUSIASM AND ENERGY.

- You are connected and in alignment with God.
- You are excited, confident, motivated and active.
- You relish the challenges of life.
- Your zest is internally driven.

> **FAR RIGHT (RED ZONE): YOUR ZEST IS OVER THE TOP AND TOO MUCH OF A GOOD THING.**

- You do not appear real to others.
- You are difficult to relate to.
- You lack a genuine affect.
- You try to create the false impression of being a high-energy mover and shaker.
- You present yourself as a power person to be reckoned with, but you are not feeling it. Your appearance is fake.
- You abandon critical thinking in favor of feeling enthusiastic.

CONSIDER THIS!

E *When you choose to use the tool, Zest, you are choosing to have excitement, motivation, creativity and inspiration in your life.*

T *The bottom line with this tool is to keep it real. God wants us to be authentic. Do give 100% of what you have and remember that zest must dance with authenticity. Giving 100% means approaching every day with excitement and energy.*

WHAT AREAS IN MY LIFE ARE LACKING ZEST, ENTHUSIASM AND ENERGY?

My *intention* is to choose and apply *zest, enthusiasm* and *energy* to all areas of my life.

Today, I want to take responsibility for choosing to use the tool, ZEST, ENTHUSIASM and ENERGY.

Here are the ways in which I can *walk with zest, enthusiasm* and *energy* with God in the Green Zone.

PERSONAL:

FAMILY:

WORK:

SOCIAL:

FAITH:

I will walk in the Green Zone with God today by choosing to use the tool ZEST, ENTHUSIASM and ENERGY.

"But the fruit of the Spirit is love, joy, peace, patience, kindness, goodness, faithfulness."
GALATIANS 5:22

"Be kind and compassionate to one another, forgiving each other, just as in Christ God forgave you."
EPHESIANS 4:32

"Remember this: Whoever sows sparingly will also reap sparingly, and whoever sows generously will also reap generously."
2 CORINTHIANS 9:6

13　KINDNESS and GENEROSITY

Kindness is a character tool from which the other character tools flow. It is a simple yet profound virtue with a far-reaching impact. Warm memories are frequently associated with small yet powerful acts of kindness. Our personal and professional relationships change and grow by the caring and compassionate action of others. Being kind means placing the needs of others above your own for the betterment of everyone involved.

Generosity involves giving from the heart without a price tag. Being generous means giving without the expectation of receiving anything in return.

Kindness and generosity are motivated by a care and concern for others. By definition, they are devoid of the assurance of reciprocity, a gain in reputation or other self-benefit.

Acts of kindness reshape our self-image, promote healthy and strong relationships and cultivate peace, contentment and satisfaction in our lives. Scientific research clearly demonstrates that providing an act of kindness boosts not only our immune system but also our production of serotonin. It is amazing that not only does the person providing the act of kindness benefit from increased serotonin levels but so do the people receiving that act of kindness. What is even more amazing is that people simply observing this act of kindness benefit as well!

Take a moment to recall when someone extended kindness or generosity to you. Now recall a time when you witnessed an act of kindness or generosity. Finally, recall a time when you extended an act of kindness or generosity toward others. How did these acts of kindness affect you? We hope that an act of kindness and generosity, whether given, received or observed, has inexplicably warmed your heart!

E *I believe that when we exercise kindness and generosity we are instantly put into a perspective to focus on others. Kindness and generosity inspire us to look at others in regard to the impact that our words and our* *behaviors have on them. If you want to lift up and inspire others, reach for the tool, "Kindness and Generosity." Kindness and generosity inspires kindness and generosity in others.*

T *I believe that when I choose to be kind and generous to my wife, my children, my customers and employees, I feel more connected with them. For example, I feel uplifted when I spend more time listening to a problem my customer may have at that moment, than I do focusing on business. The business will be taken care of at some point. However, the time I spend listening to that person about the problem they may have is priceless. Just being there to listen creates a bond that is invaluable in my relationship with that customer.*

GAUGING YOUR KINDNESS and GENEROSITY
Where do you measure up?

FAR LEFT (RED ZONE): YOU ARE NOT SENSITIVE TO OTHERS NEEDS.

- You are only focused on your own needs.
- You are stingy and self-centered.
- You are apathetic.
- You exhibit a lack of caring.
- You have a mean attitude.

THE MIDDLE (GREEN ZONE): YOU ARE KIND AND GENEROUS.

- You are connected and in alignment with God.
- You extend kindness and generosity without any expectations.
- You serve and give to others without any expectations.

- You use kindness and generosity to manipulate others for self-centered and self-serving purposes.
- Your kindness is at the expense of someone else.
- Your kindness is at the expense of you and/or your family.

CONSIDER THIS!

E *Why be kind and generous? Because acts of kindness promote happiness and well-being! I believe that to be good at anything –including using the tool kindness and generosity –you have to practice it. Practice, in this case, means that each day you challenge yourself to look for opportunities to extend kindness and generosity without any strings attached.*

T *My Christian faith asks me to place myself in a position of servitude to others. When I assume an attitude of service to others, I find that the tool, Kindness and Generosity, is invaluable.*

IF I WERE TO BE KIND AND GENEROUS TODAY, I WOULD CHOOSE TO.....

My *intention* is to choose and apply *kindness* and *generosity*
to all areas of my life.

Today, I want to *take responsibility* for choosing to use the tool,
KINDNESS and GENEROSITY.

Here are the ways in which I *can walk in kindness* and *generosity* with God
in the Green Zone:

PERSONAL:

FAMILY:

WORK:

SOCIAL:

FAITH:

I will walk in the Green Zone with God today by choosing to use the tool,
KINDNESS and GENEROSITY.

"Then you will know the truth, and the truth will set you free."
JOHN 8:32

"Truthful lips endure forever, but a lying tongue lasts only a moment."
PROVERBS 12:19

14 HONESTY

AUTHENTICITY and GENUINENESS

When you choose to be honest, you present yourself in a genuine and authentic manner. You are transparent with your motivations, intentions and commitments. You are accountable and responsible for your emotions and behaviors.

Choosing to be honest is a choice we can make not only through our words but through our behaviors as well. It is important that our words and our behaviors match up consistently. When your words and behaviors are in alignment, you are living your life in a genuine and authentic way.

Do you feel your image and the "real you" don't match up? Are you concerned? Do you worry there might be a gap between what people see in you and who you really are? Are you two different personas?

FRONT STAGE/BACK STAGE

Does your image and the "real you" match up? Is there a gap between what people see in you and who you really are?

Front Stage is the term we use to describe how others see you. It's how you perform. It's what you want people to know about you. **Back Stage** is the term we use to describe who you truly are. Does your *Front Stage* match your *Back Stage*?

Are you honest with your words and behaviors?

If you are a parent, do you discipline and guide your children in a way that keeps you humble and true to your beliefs? Do you speak and relate to your children in a way that is genuine and caring?

Are you real with the role in life that you play? Are you doing the best you can to be real in your role as a spouse, a friend, a co-worker, a parent or an employee?

When you choose to be dishonest, you are choosing to be deceptive. It takes deception to cover deception. It is a race without a finish line. Deception comes at the cost of being in the present. If your focus is on what you need to say in order to feel or look good or if you focus on how you will respond to what people might say to you, then you have just taken a detour from authenticity.

When you choose to use character strengths like honesty and genuineness to be your authentic self, you will feel motivated and energized!

Are you strong enough to be your most authentic self?

E *For me, this tool has a 100% guarantee. Choosing to be authentic requires that I make a diligent effort to make sure that my front stage matches up with my back stage. It requires me to be honest with myself about who I am and how I want to present myself. When my front stage and my back stage are in alignment, I am authentic. When I interact with people from this level of authenticity, my level of genuineness is clear to other people. I know that each time I choose not to use this tool, I will regret my choice 100% of the time.*

T *This tool is what allows me to have a good night's sleep every night. I know that when I am honest and genuine with my actions during each day, I have presented myself as I really am and I don't have to worry about how people see me. I keep this tool in mind in all my actions and decision-making processes each day. My customers, friends and family know who I am and that they can rely on me being authentic today, tomorrow and each day in the future. It gives them confidence that they can always count on me.*

GAUGING YOUR HONESTY
Where do you measure up?

- You are driven by fear that you are not good enough, so you pretend to be what you are not.
- You have to cover up lies with other lies.
- You are deceptive.
- You are not authentic.

THE MIDDLE (GREEN ZONE): YOU ARE NATURAL AND 100% REAL.

- You are connected and in alignment with God.
- Your front stage matches your back stage.
- Your words and behaviors match up consistently.
- You are transparent with your motivations, intentions and commitments.

FAR RIGHT (RED ZONE): YOU ARE MANIPULATIVE AND SELF-FOCUSED.

- You use the appearance of being genuine to control others.
- Your honesty is at the cost of kindness and respect to others.
- You use honesty as a way to manipulate a situation or a person.

CONSIDER THIS!

EMy job as a therapist offers me the opportunity to see thousands of people. I am profoundly impacted every day by how toxic and cancerous deception can be in our relationships and our lives. Deception presents itself in every session in some form whether it is an individual, a couple or a family. People believe it is easier to be deceptive than it is to risk being honest and showing their true authentic self. We have morphed into a culture that believes and accepts that it is easier to be deceptive than it is to be honest.

However, I can tell you that from my experience, people do crave authenticity and honesty, both within themselves as well as in their relationships. I want to inspire you to take the risk to use this tool today. It is the one tool that will give you instant results both internally and externally. You will find that authenticity is contagious in your relationships.

T *Strive to walk with God in the Green Zone. Being who you really are is a challenge in today's society. Everyone thinks they need to be someone else. The grass is always greener on the other side. I guarantee that if you choose to use this tool in all aspects of your life, you will be on your way to finding the peace, satisfaction and contentment you seek.*

LIST THREE CHARACTERISTICS OF MY *FRONT* STAGE SELF and then, LIST THREE CHARACTERISTICS OF MY *BACK* STAGE SELF:

My *intention* is to choose and apply *honesty* to all areas of my life.

Today, I want to *take responsibility* for choosing to use the tool, HONESTY.

Here are the ways in which I can *walk in honesty* with God
in the Green Zone:

PERSONAL:

FAMILY:

WORK:

SOCIAL:

FAITH:

I will walk in the Green Zone with God today by choosing to use the tool,
HONESTY.

"Blessed is the man who perseveres under trial, because when he has stood the test, he will receive the crown of life that God has promised to those who love him."
JAMES 1:12

"Let us not become weary in doing good, for at the proper time we will reap a harvest if we do not give up."
GALATIANS 6:9

15 PERSEVERANCE
INDUSTRY and DILIGENCE

Perseverance means you finish what you start. You are industrious and prepared to take on difficult projects and follow through to completion. Perseverance requires drive, energy and action.

```
DRIVE + ENERGY + ACTION = PERSEVERANCE

                Dedication
               Determination
                Endurance
                Persistence
                  Stamina
               Steadfastness
                  Tenacity
```

In our culture, we have a big problem with patience and perseverance. We expect instant results. When we are hungry, we want food...fast. Hence, fast food. When we are feeling uncomfortable, we look for an immediate way to feel better. We call this "instant gratification."

Perseverance is the direct opposite of instant gratification. Perseverance requires us to stay focused. When we choose perseverance, we choose to move forward despite the obstacles or the discomfort that often side-track us.

Many of the obstacles we experience in our lives revolve around relationships. Instant gratification gives us permission to walk away or deny that there are conflicts/obstacles in our relationships. We believe that when there is a problem, it is easier to walk away than to confront and push through the issues. We are only concerned about what is going to make us feel good right now. As we walk away from confrontations, we often find ourselves walking toward drugs, alcohol, pornography, gambling, etc.

Our relationships are never absent of times where we want to give up, turn our back or walk away. These are the times when perseverance will get you through any tough situation. Our relationships are worth fighting for! It is too easy to turn our backs and look for the easy fix instead of pushing forward and investing in a resolution. Perseverance is the answer when we feel like giving up.

When people are admired for their "survivor" skills, it's because of their ability to keep moving forward in life, in spite of obstacles in the way. They keep pace, one foot in front of the other, staying in motion in spite of circumstances that would make many individuals freeze in place.

What do you do when life throws you a curve? Do you have the energy and drive to keep on living or do you stop short in your tracks? Do you curl up in the fetal position, wanting someone to wake you when the problem is over? Do you hope someone will care enough to "rescue" you by telling you what to do or step in to help you until you get on your feet again?

When you choose to persevere, you are choosing to focus on the here and now because you can only persevere in that moment. Your life becomes satisfying and more peaceful than it would have been if you had allowed yourself to "cave in" during the crisis. It's a good idea to be mindful of what we teach our children. It's important to show them how to keep going in spite of a problem. When you persevere, you keep things going in spite of what may stand in your way.

E *In my personal life, I view my relationships like a cage fight. Cage fights are interesting because no one is allowed to leave until the fight is over. There are no exits. Fighters must draw deep within themselves because they know there are no other options except for resolution. My marriage, my relationships with my children, my relationships with my family and friends have no exits.*

One of my favorite quotes about perseverance is..."If I had to select one quality, one personal characteristic that I regard as being most highly correlated with success, whatever the field, I would pick the trait of persistence. Determination. The will to endure to the end, to get knocked down seventy times and get up off the floor saying. "Here comes number seventy-one!" (Richard M. Devos, co-founder Amway)

T *I believe that success in life is very simple. It is never quitting or giving up. It is simply showing up each day and doing the best job I can at living up to the responsibilities God has given me. Doing this leaves me satisfied and content.*

GAUGING YOUR PERSEVERENCE
Where do you measure up?

FAR LEFT (RED ZONE): YOU QUIT. YOU GIVE UP.

- You choose to not finish or complete difficult tasks.
- You procrastinate, getting less done.
- You're in the fetal position, seeing yourself as helpless and powerless.
- You deny or do not resolve conflicts in your relationships.

THE MIDDLE (GREEN ZONE): YOU PERSEVERE.

- You are connected and in alignment with God.
- You work until the job is done.
- You take pride in completing tasks.
- You focus on a specific task and stay directed.
- You push through conflicts in your relationships by using healthy confrontation.

FAR RIGHT (RED ZONE): YOU PERSEVERE IN AN UNHEALTHY MANNER.

- You persevere at an unhealthy cost to yourself.
- You persevere at the cost of someone else.
- You persevere for self-serving purposes.

CONSIDER THIS!

(E) *Perseverance seems like a harder tool to introduce to people. People are programmed by our culture to seek out anything that is going to make us feel better right now. We are smothered by a variety of ways to gain instant gratification. The idea to delay pleasure or to push through discomfort is difficult for people to wrap their heads around.*

Perseverance is one of the most important character tools that you can have in your tool box. Perseverance is the fuel that will drive you to get better at using all the other tools. Perseverance does not necessarily mean that you will have successful completion of a task. It does mean that you will continue to move forward towards resolution.

(T) *Perseverance is the character tool where you choose to focus on the present and move forward... rather than being motivated and influenced by whatever your limiting emotion is at that moment.*

THREE AREAS IN MY LIFE WHERE I CAN BENEFIT FROM USING THE CHARACTER TOOL, PERSEVERANCE, ARE.....

My intention is to choose and apply perseverance to all areas of my life.

Today, I want to take responsibility for choosing to use the tool, PERSEVERANCE.

Here are the ways in which I can walk with perseverance with God in the Green Zone:

PERSONAL:

FAMILY:

WORK:

SOCIAL:

FAITH:

I will walk in the Green Zone with God today by choosing to use the tool, PERSEVERANCE.

"Love is patient, love is kind. It does not envy, it does not boast, it is not proud. It is not rude, it is not self-seeking, it is not easily angered, it keeps no record of wrongs. Love does not delight in evil but rejoices with the truth. It always protects, always trusts, always hopes, always perseveres."

1 CORINTHIANS 13:4-7

16 UNCONDITIONAL LOVE

Our ability to choose to love unconditionally is the character tool that ties all of us together regardless of our religion, ethnic or socio-economic group. Do the people you love know how much you love them? Do you allow the people in your life to love you?

Love expresses itself in four different ways in a relationship. One expression of love is from the individual who is our primary source of affection, protection and care. A second form of love is for the individual we depend on for safety and security. The third form of love is the love that involves our passionate desire for emotional, physical, or sexual intimacy with an individual. The fourth expression of love is the love that we give and receive to people that we encounter and interact with in our lives.

The goal for all these expressions of love is that we love unconditionally. No strings attached!

Love fuels passion, hope and desire. It generates creativity and gives us purpose, making us feel alive. When we think of love, we typically think of romantic love, yet love can be expressed in a variety of ways –all unique, fulfilling and enriching our lives.

We all want to feel loved. We think about it, hope for it, fantasize about it, go to great lengths to achieve it, and believe that our lives are incomplete without it. The lack of unconditional love in our lives is the cause of most of our anger and confusion. It is no exaggeration to say that our emotional need for unconditional love is just as great as our physical need for air and food.

We cannot experience unconditional love until we first choose to love people unconditionally. Unconditional love is choosing to love without any strings attached.

Choosing to love unconditionally fills us with happiness and makes us feel whole!

E *As a marriage and family therapist, I have found that relationships can involve more than one kind of love. They can start as one expression of love, and evolve into another over time. It is up to us to recognize and act upon the different kinds of love in our life. We cultivate this unique love and promote emotional well-being through our connections with our family members, friends, neighbors, and even pets!*

T *I believe that the capacity to love and to be loved is easily transferrable into the work place. Imagine what the work world might look like if more people demonstrated the capacity to love and be loved. Employees would feel truly appreciated rather than feeling taken for granted. Employees would feel more connected to each other rather than isolated from each other. And, employees might view each other as friends rather than competitors or enemies. I apply all these principles in my family business and it gives us a closer relationship with our customers, which in turn makes us more successful.*

GAUGING YOUR LOVE OF LEARNING
Where do you measure up?

> **FAR LEFT (RED ZONE): YOU CHOOSE NOT TO LOVE OR BE LOVED.**

- You believe you are "damaged goods" without the capacity to love or to be loved.
- You believe you are "empty" and cannot give or receive love.
- You believe you are permanently "broken" and "damaged" by your life experiences.

- You believe you are alone, isolated and cannot give what you do not have.
- You easily withhold love and end relationships when your expectations are not met.

THE MIDDLE (GREEN ZONE): YOU VALUE CLOSE RELATIONSHIPS AND CONNECTIONS WITH OTHERS.

- You are connected and in alignment with God.
- You express love without the expectation of getting anything in return.
- You choose to demonstrate love.
- You allow the people in your life to love you.
- You communicate to the people in your life how much you love them.
- You accept expressions of love from those around you at face value.

FAR RIGHT (RED ZONE): YOU CHOOSE NOT TO LOVE UNCONDITIONALLY.

- You manipulate others with your love and your need for love comes at an unhealthy cost to others.
- You accept being in an unhealthy relationship without regard to the effect it has on everyone else in the family.
- You trade physical or emotional abuse for love.

CONSIDER THIS!

E *Love begins with YOU! It is hard to feel worthy of love if someone is criticizing you all the time; especially, if that someone is your inner voice talking in your head. Stop comparing yourself to others and feeling like you are helpless and powerless.*

It is important that you open up your eyes and see the variety of ways that people communicate their love to you. When someone looks out for you, empathizes with you, stands up for you, listens to you, relates to you, appreciates you, respects you, accepts you, or acknowledges you, they are giving you love!

When someone thanks you, encourages you, believes in you, supports you, forgives you, soothes you, uplifts you, or trusts you, they are giving you love! When someone opens up to you, tries to know you, stays strong for you, assumes the best in you, compliments you, mentors you, makes time for you, or makes an effort for you, they are giving you love!

Love is always coming at us, in one form or another—sometimes from friends, sometimes from family, sometimes from strangers we may only know in passing. It might be a thoughtful call at just the right time, a spontaneous warm hug or an inspirational comment on a blog on a day when you felt weak and afraid. We all have so much love to give, and we're giving it every day. The only question is whether or not we are also able to recognize and really receive it.

T *I believe if you want to be loved, God wants you to love first. Reach out to others. Talk. Open up and reveal your feelings. Act lovingly. If someone you care about does not return your feelings, you can still act lovingly. You are responsible only for your own actions. This way there are no regrets. Giving unconditional love will bring peace, contentment and satisfaction to your life. It all begins with love!*

DO THE PEOPLE IN YOUR LIFE KNOW HOW MUCH YOU LOVE THEM? If the answer is "no," then who do you need to talk to today to tell them how much you love them?

My *intention* is to choose and apply *unconditional love* to all areas of my life.

Today, I want to *take responsibility* for choosing to use the tool,
UNCONDITIONAL LOVE.

Here are the ways in which I can *walk in unconditional love* with God
in the Green Zone:

PERSONAL:

FAMILY:

WORK:

SOCIAL

FAITH:

I will walk in the Green Zone with God today by choosing to use the tool,
UNCONDITIONAL LOVE.

"Let the wise hear and add to their learning and let the discerning get guidance."
PROVERBS 1:5

"The heart of the discerning acquires knowledge, the ears of the wise seek it out."
PROVERBS 18:15

17 A LOVE OF LEARNING
BE A STUDENT OF LIFE

A love of learning is the excitement, anticipation and curiosity of learning new skills, acquiring new knowledge or building on our existing skills and knowledge. A love of learning is an awareness of the endless flow of information that we are absorbing daily – minute by minute. A love of learning is the processing of that information and how it impacts or influences us, and ultimately, what we do with it.

A love of learning also encompasses the desire to take all of life's experiences, positive or negative, and learn from them. We need to see all life challenges as opportunities for us to learn and grow from rather than perceiving them as personal attacks. We need to look for the good and bad in all situations and understand what we can from these circumstances so we are better equipped to handle the next crisis or challenge. We are the culmination of all of our life experiences and how we use those experiences is in direct correlation to the happiness and success we are seeking.

A love of learning is something we should practice as adults and absolutely instill in our children! It begins with role modeling and book knowledge and spills over into the areas of socialization and relationships. We typically want to protect our children and shield them from experiences that would probably make them stronger individuals in the end. Modeling a love of learning helps your child understand that when uncomfortable situations arise, they too, can actually learn from them. This philosophy will help carry them through childhood and into adulthood.

The benefits of loving to learn during the school years are obvious. Students who love to learn are more likely to engage in their schoolwork and receive positive feedback from teachers and parents. However, the benefits of this strength extend beyond the school years and into retirement. "Indeed, a love of learning may be particularly valuable during older age in that it may prevent cognitive decline. Research suggests that individuals who are able to develop and maintain interests later in life are likely to be more physically and mentally healthy than their less-engaged peers." (Krapp & Lewalter, 2001; Renninger & Shumar, 2002; Snowdon, 2001).

E *When I choose to use this tool, it allows me to look at each situation from the perspective that there is something for me to learn at that given moment. It forces me to be present focusing on what it is I'm supposed to be learning. I know that when I come from this perspective, I engage people in a way that they are clear that my focus and emotional availability is solely focused on them.*

T *A love of learning to me began with my first job in the insurance industry. My boss told me that I was going to be faced with lots of interesting challenges and experiences in this job and that I needed to learn something from each and every one of them. He said that in life I might face both good and bad challenges that come from both good and bad people. He added that it would be important to look at each personal experience and to file it away in my mental file cabinet under the heading of "good" and "bad." We will have a tendency to want to disregard the bad and only learn from the good things that happen. Learning from the bad things in life helps me avoid making mistakes that I've made before. All of my experiences make me who I am. The true value comes from what I've learned from those experiences.*

GAUGING YOUR LOVE OF LEARNING
Where do you measure up?

- You choose to survive instead of thrive.
- You choose not to appreciate the wisdom you have already acquired through your own experiences.
- You choose to not ask for help or look for resources.

- You are connected and in alignment with God.
- You are motivated to go from situation to situation, confident in your ability to assess what each situation has in store for you.
- You understand that you learn from each experience.
- You see your take-away lessons clearly.
- You are "in the moment—you are real."
- You are a student of life and all its lessons. You crave learning.
- You understand that being a student of life demands that you choose humility and sincerity.
- You see each situation as an opportunity not only to learn but to do better the next time. You seek opportunities for self-improvement.

- You act as if you have all the answers to cover the truth of feeling insecure.
- You present yourself as if you are excited about learning and that you are a student of life, while you really believe that you already have all the answers.
- You believe you won't be accepted if you don't have all the answers so you present yourself as a "know-it-all".
- You are not open to learning from others.

CONSIDER THIS!

E I walk the walk by applying these character tools. When counseling children and adolescents, I say, "I want to know what things look like through your eyes." At the end of a session, I ask them to tell me one thing they wish was a little different about our time together.

I say, "I ask you because I want to learn from you, too." This process falls under the heading of "A love of learning." The kids tell me they enjoy my asking them about themselves. They feel heard and understood by me wanting to know how things look to them. The kids feel valued. Children understand this concept even as young as four and five years of age. They can tell if I am "killing time" by my questions or if I really want to learn.

Are you genuinely interested in others, wanting to know more of their stories rather than telling your own? Are you aware of how you impact people when you show real interest in them? People are generally savvy, picking up on cues and are drawn to people who are interested in them.

My wife, Leslie says, "I feel that life is something that should be approached from the standpoint that we are always the student, moment to moment, from birth to death. Life always has a fresh restart. You will always be learning because there is always something new to learn."

T I am a student of life. I have to be in order to survive the constant changes that occur in my chosen profession. To me, a love of learning means trying to be present each day in all of my relationships. When I am present and connected with God, I have life clarity. When I am operating in the present, I see the bigger picture of what I observe and I see how I can be a positive influence in the relationships around me.

AS A STUDENT OF LIFE, WHAT THREE POSITIVES OR TAKEAWAY POINTS CAN YOU SEE IN A NEGATIVE SITUATION THAT YOU ARE IN RIGHT NOW?

My *intention* is to choose and apply *a love of learning* to all areas of my life.

Today, I want to *take responsibility* for choosing to use the tool,
A LOVE OF LEARNING.

Here are the ways in which I can *walk in love for learning* with God
in the Green Zone:

PERSONAL:

FAMILY:

WORK:

SOCIAL:

FAITH:

I will walk in the Green Zone with God today by choosing to use the tool,
A LOVE OF LEARNING.

"For whoever exalts himself will be humbled, and whoever humbles himself will be exalted."
MATTHEW 23:12

"Do nothing out of selfish ambition or vain conceit, but in humility consider others better than yourselves. Each of you should look not only to your own interests, but also to the interests of others. Your attitude should be the same as that of Christ Jesus."
PHILIPPIANS 2:3-5

18 HUMILITY

The quality of humility is marked by modesty, peacefulness, quietness and an unassuming attitude. The opposite of humility is arrogance and pride. In today's culture, pride is celebrated and arrogance is almost a prerequisite to be taken seriously in business, politics and sports.

We often think that humility is only for wimps and losers. This is because we misunderstand the true meaning of humility. When we choose humility, we are placing the needs of our families, our work places and social circles above our own. This means that we are actively searching for opportunities to serve others and lift them up.

There is a difference between the strength in humility and the perceived strength in arrogance.

HUMILITY VS. ARROGANCE

- Humility learns; arrogance knows.
- Humility listens; arrogance talks.
- Humility serves others; arrogance serves ourselves.
- Humility builds others up. Arrogance builds ourselves up.
- Humility joins; arrogance stands aloof.
- Humility connects; arrogance disconnects.
- Humility enables us to ask, "How can I help?

E *A statement I commonly make to people is, "Those who know, don't talk and those who talk, don't know." It is all about striking a healthy balance between humility and confidence. In other words, I have enough confidence in myself to lift others up without needing recognition for doing so.*

My Peaceful Pete story: In my mid-twenties, I was a young gun regional marketing director responsible for teaching insurance agents to sell insurance. At the end of the year, they called all of us young corporate guys into a meeting to teach us to be better managers. In one segment of the meeting, they drew a line on the floor. At one end was a silhouette of a weak looking individual called "Peaceful Pete." At the other end of the line was a macho-looking individual called "Hardass Hank." Our class facilitator asked us all to choose where we fit on that line regarding our management techniques. As I was working with a number of young studs, there was a big fight to place themselves somewhere on that line between the middle and "Hardass Hank." Everyone thought that being a "Hardass Hank" was a better way of being a successful manager. In this process, I was pushed to the end of the line closest to "Peaceful Pete." I was humiliated. Everyone looked at me as weak in my management skills.

Now that I am 50-years-old and look back on my life of being a "Peaceful Pete," I realize that this is exactly where I was supposed to be. I see strength in humility and take joy in seeing and helping others succeed.

GAUGING YOUR HUMILITY
Where do you measure up?

FAR LEFT (RED ZONE): YOU DON'T EXERCISE HUMILITY IN YOUR DAILY LIFE.

- You are arrogant.
- You are a braggart.
- You are not interested in serving others.

- You are connected and in alignment with God.
- You do not brag.
- You understand that you are not the center of the universe.
- You do not regard yourself as superior to others.
- You let your accomplishments speak for themselves.
- You refuse to "one-up" others in relationships.
- You avoid flaunting or seeking to be the center of attention.
- You take joy in lifting others up and seeing them succeed.

- You use the appearance of humility with the intention of manipulating others.
- You use the appearance of humility for self-serving purposes.
- You use humility at the cost of others.
- You confuse humility by presenting yourself as passive or having low esteem.

CONSIDER THIS!

EYou can better understand and apply humility by looking at humility in three different ways. First, you understand that the universe is larger than just meeting your individual wants and needs. Secondly, humility is your ability to serve others with no strings attached. Finally, serving others makes you a stronger person. Humility is the outcome when you recognize and acknowledge that you cannot do it on your own. It's the point when you connect with God. You invite God into your life because you realize you cannot do it on your own.

TWhen you choose to use humility, it gives you a whole different vantage point from which to view your world. Humility allows you to sit back and take in everything that is going on in a conversation or situation without feeling the need to say something. It allows you to assess all the different needs and characteristics of the situation that is going on and look for the proper entry point to help and lift people up. It truly allows you to see things for the way they really are.

TODAY, I CAN PRACTICE HUMILITY IN MY RELATIONSHIPS WITH THE PEOPLE IN MY LIFE BY.....

My *intention* is to choose and apply *humility* to all areas of my life.

Today, I want to *take responsibility* for choosing to use the tool, HUMILITY.

Here are the ways in which I can *walk in humility* with God in the Green Zone:

PERSONAL:

FAMILY:

WORK:

SOCIAL:

FAITH:

I will walk in the Green Zone with God today by choosing to use the tool, HUMILITY.

"Be joyful in hope, patient in affliction, faithful in prayer."
ROMANS 12:12

"Now faith is being sure of what we hope for and certain of what we do not see."
HEBREWS 11:1

"May the God of hope fill you with all joy and peace as you trust in him, so that you may overflow with hope by the power of the Holy Spirit."
ROMANS 15:13

19   RESILIENCY

Resiliency is the ability to recover from stress and adversity. Resilient people are flexible, positive and project a degree of confidence. Resiliency allows us to get through daily stress and life challenges. Resilient people are able to recover from difficult situations without lasting effects and difficulties. In fact, the more resilient you are, the more quickly you are able to recover from situations that would pull the rug out from under those with little resiliency.

In today's culture, there is a tendency to blame others for our miseries and suffering. We assume the victim role with this mind-set, which is the exact opposite of resiliency. When we are in a victim role, our focus is on blaming others for where we are or how we feel in a given moment. We do not take any responsibility or accountability. Therefore, we feel we have no choice or control in the outcome. At this point, we are waiting for somebody to say or do something to resolve our struggle because we cannot do it ourselves. "I need to wait for you to apologize or make amends with me before I can move forward." As a consequence, it takes away our initiative to be resilient and create the outcome we desire.

When we choose resiliency, we have the ability to experience negative and positive situations and find redeeming qualities and opportunities in both. We look at the challenges we face as opportunities for us to grow as individuals. We find it is better to move toward the pain searching for opportunities to learn instead of running or hiding from it. This is where you believe that adversity should be dealt with head-on and see the value of choosing resiliency. Resilience is the process of adapting to difficult or challenging life experiences, says the late Al Siebert, PhD, founder of The Resiliency Center in Portland, Oregon. Curious to know how your own resilience rates? Take this quiz, adapted from Siebert's book.

The Resiliency Advantage.

Rate yourself from 1-5 (1 = strongly disagree 5 = strongly agree):

1) I'm usually optimistic. I see difficulties as temporary and expect to overcome them.
2) Feelings of anger, loss and discouragement don't last long.
3) I can tolerate high levels of ambiguity and uncertainty about situations.
4) I adapt quickly to new developments. I'm curious. I ask questions.
5) I'm playful. I find the humor in rough situations, and can laugh at myself.
6) I learn valuable lessons from my experiences and from the experiences of others.
7) I'm good at solving problems. I'm good at making things work well.
8) I'm strong and durable. I hold up well during tough times.
9) I've converted misfortune into good luck and found benefits in bad experiences.

Less than 20: Low Resilience — You may have trouble handling pressure or setbacks, and may feel deeply hurt by any criticism. When things don't go well, you may feel helpless and without hope. Consider seeking some professional counsel or support in developing your resiliency skills. Connect with others who share your developmental goals.

20–30: Some Resilience — You have some valuable pro-resiliency skills, but also plenty of room for improvement. Strive to strengthen the characteristics you already have and to cultivate the characteristics you lack. You may also wish to seek some outside coaching or support.

30–35: Adequate Resilience — You are a self-motivated learner who recovers well from most challenges. Learning more about resilience, and consciously building your resiliency skills, will empower you to find more joy in life, even in the face of adversity.

35–45: Highly Resilient — You bounce back well from life's setbacks and can thrive even under pressure. You could be of service to others who are trying to cope better with adversity.

E *When I choose resiliency, I am reminding myself to be focused on the present and what is in front of me that I can change rather than continuing to focus on aspects that I cannot change. When I choose resiliency, I am consciously choosing to move forward.*

T *I pray each day for the ability to choose to be resilient. Without resiliency, I would not be able to live up to my daily responsibilities and take care of those who count on me. I feel that being resilient is the key to success. To be resilient requires a degree of courage as well. It is what allows me to "step back into the batter box" after being hit, so to speak. Being in sales has required a degree of resiliency as an emotional safety net. I know that every "no" means I'm that much closer to a "yes".*

GAUGING YOUR RESILIENCY
Where do you measure up?

FAR LEFT (RED ZONE): YOU CHOOSE TO HAVE A VICTIM

- You choose to not recover from stress or life crises.
- You choose to not forgive or accept the past.
- You choose to focus on injustice and revenge.
- You choose to not take risks.

- You are connected and in alignment with God.
- You learn from mistakes instead of denying they ever happened.
- You see obstacles as challenges you can navigate around.
- You use adversity and obstacles as a means to make you stronger.
- You face challenges head-on rather than seeing yourself as helpless and powerless – a victim of those challenges.

- You choose to move forward without taking your family's needs or emotions into consideration.
- You say to yourself, "I'm going to do what I want at all costs".
- Your forward movement does not honor or value the magnitude of the situation.
- You plow ahead without paying attention to what needs to be dealt with or learned.

CONSIDER THIS!

E *When you choose to be resilient, you are choosing to be connected with God. You are not just going through the motions of life. You believe in the bigger picture where everything you experience in your life is moving you towards something greater.*

T *Resiliency is another one of those little secrets of success in life. Being resilient allows you to keep plodding, putting one foot in front of the other even when you don't want to and feel there is no way you can go forward. Going forward through life's challenges with resiliency makes you strong and confident that no matter what happens, everything will be okay. Going through life knowing everything will be okay will give you the peace, contentment and satisfaction that you are looking for.*

IF I WERE MORE RESILIENT IN MY LIFE, I WOULD.....

My intention is to choose and apply resiliency to all areas of my life.

Today, I want to take responsibility for choosing to use the tool, RESILIENCY.

Here are the ways in which I can walk with resiliency with God
in the Green Zone:

PERSONAL:

FAMILY:

WORK:

SOCIAL:

FAITH:

I will walk in the Green Zone with God today by choosing to use the tool,
RESILIENCY.

"The man of integrity walks securely, but he who takes crooked paths will be found out."
PROVERBS 10:9

"Better a poor man whose walk is blameless than a rich man whose ways are perverse."
PROVERBS 28:6

"Better a poor man whose walk is blameless than a fool whose lips are perverse."
PROVERBS 19:1

20 INTEGRITY

Integrity can be defined as an adherence to a code of moral values, principles and character tools. Integrity speaks to demonstrating a consistency in your actions that are in alignment with your personal values and principles.

Integrity is speaking the truth and presenting oneself in a genuine way. Integrity is being open and honest about your own thoughts, emotions and responsibilities. Integrity is being very careful to not mislead others through your actions or your failure to act. Integrity is presenting yourself as the same person regardless of who is in front of you. Integrity can be summed up simply as doing the right thing for the right reason even when no one is watching.

THE INTEGRITY METER

Consider this tool as an integrity meter or a gauge which indicates your level of integrity. This integrity meter is similar to a voltage meter that all good carpenters keep in their tool box. The voltage meter is important to the carpenter because it helps him/her make sure that the power flowing through the house has the correct voltage. When your home has the correct voltage running through it, everything works at its optimum performance.

This voltage meter is analogous to your integrity meter because the more character tools that you integrate into your life, the higher your integrity meter rates. The higher your integrity meter rates, the more you are operating at your optimum performance. For you to operate at optimum performance, you must strive to be in the green zone of every tool that you use. The more character tools that you utilize in the green zone every day, the more peace, contentment and satisfaction you will have in your daily life.

E *I believe that integrity is the integration of all our character tools into our daily lives. It is my experience as a therapist that the integrity of families, marriages and all the encompassing relationships is driven by the degree of the integrity of each person. When everyone exercises a high degree of integrity, relationships are at their strongest and healthiest.*

*I believe that integrity is a culmination of all the tools in the **Timeless Twenty Toolkit©**. It is imperative for us to strive to use as many of these tools in our daily lives as possible. I believe that when you add integrity to a sincere desire to lift up those around you, you will experience the happiness you are looking for. Integrity simply means that you are looking at all the responsibilities in your life and living up to them the best you possibly can.*

GAUGING YOUR INTEGRITY
Where do you measure up?

FAR LEFT (RED ZONE): YOU ARE DISHONEST AND CHOOSE NOT TO USE CHARACTER TOOLS.

- You are dishonest.
- You are untrustworthy-your words and behaviors do not match.
- You are inconsistent and unpredictable.
- You are unethical.

THE MIDDLE (GREEN ZONE): YOU ARE UTILIZING ALL YOUR CHARACTER TOOLS IN THE GREEN ZONE.

- You are connected and in alignment with God.
- You are the same person no matter who is looking.
- You make healthy choices even when you don't think someone is watching you.
- You are trustworthy.
- People learn they can rely on you.
- Your choices support your values and goals so that you are not sabotaging your better self.

- Your words and actions are at the cost of someone else.
- You are 100% bluntly honest without utilizing empathy and sensitivity.

CONSIDER THIS!

E *Your integrity is your golden egg. Choosing to use each of these character strengths when no one is looking and when you know you won't get any credit for it is when you are at your strongest. The more character tools you choose to use, the higher level of integrity you have and the stronger you are as a person.*

T *As the rebar is the strength of your home's foundation, character tools are the strength of your personal foundation. The strength of your personal foundation is called integrity. The more integrity you have, the stronger your foundation. The stronger your foundation, the stronger your relationships. The stronger your relationships, the more peace, contentment and satisfaction you will experience in life.*

THREE AREAS IN MY LIFE THAT WOULD BENEFIT FROM ME CHOOSING INTEGRITY ARE.....

My *intention* is to choose and apply *integrity* to all areas of my life.

Today, I want to *take responsibility* for choosing to use the tool, INTEGRITY.

Here are the ways in which I can *walk with integrity* with God in the Green Zone:

PERSONAL:

FAMILY:

WORK:

SOCIAL:

FAITH:

I will walk in the Green Zone with God today by choosing to use the tool, INTEGRITY.

OUR INVITATION TO YOU

Now that you have learned about the **Timeless Twenty Character Tools©**, you can imagine the benefits you will experience when you choose to use them! Clearly, if you choose not to use the Timeless Twenty you will be operating in the red zone, and you will experience instability, uncertainty and hopelessness in your life.

Choosing to use the **Timeless Twenty Character Tools©** and shooting for the Green Zone with each tool, will manifest the peace, contentment and satisfaction you desire to promote healthy and happy relationships in your life.

YOU WILL EXPERIENCE STRENGTH AND HOPE EVEN IN THE FACE OF UNCERTAINTY

"Trust in the Lord with all your heart, and do not lean on your own understanding. In all your ways acknowledge him, and he will make straight your paths." **(Proverbs 3:5-6)**

"For I know the plans I have for you," declares the LORD, *" plans to prosper you and not to harm you, plans to give you hope and a future."* **(Jeremiah 29:11)**

"For everything that was written in the past was written to teach us, so that through endurance and the encouragement of the Scriptures we might have hope." **(Romans 15:4)**

When you are operating in the green zone, you are choosing hope. When you are choosing hope, you are reminded to stop, be present, and listen to

God. Hope allows us to exercise humility because it requires us to acknowledge that we cannot do it on our own. We need God!

Sometimes, in our uncertainty, we struggle in truly feeling connected with God. However, when we are in the *Green Zone*, we receive an endless ocean of strength through our connection and alignment with God! Knowing this and having applicable tools to apply it are two different things. We want you to know that if you follow God's word, you will be stronger!

The character tools were specifically chosen to reinforce this belief. For example, many of Erik's clients didn't realize they had the choice to choose courage in the face of uncertainty and use it as a tool to bring *certainty* back into perspective! Remember, you too have the choice to choose hope and optimism as you walk your path with God.

Your response to uncertainty impacts everyone around you and most importantly your relationships. Choosing to shoot for the Green Zone with applicable user friendly tools will help you navigate the challenges and uncertainties in life.

These Timeless Twenty Character Tools© enable you to be mindful and thoughtful about how you are responding to uncertainty in your life. The more character tools that you choose to use in your relationships each day, the less uncertainty you will face in those relationships.

Do you realize there is a direct correlation between using the Timeless Twenty Character Tools© and your self-confidence? Self-confidence develops because of the belief that no matter what comes your way or how it unfolds, you have the tools to make it through anything. This self-confidence is grounded in our faith in God and it is what gives us strength and hope even in the face of uncertainty.

YOU WILL BUILD A FOUNDATION OF STRENGTH FOR YOUR FAMILY, THOSE AROUND YOU, AND YOURSELF

"Everyone then who hears these words of mine and does them will be like a wise man who built his house on the rock. And the rain fell, and the

floods came, and the winds blew and beat on that house, but it did not fall, because it had been founded on the rock. And everyone who hears these words of mine and does not do them will be like a foolish man who built his house on the sand. And the rain fell, and the floods came, and the winds blew and beat against that house, and it fell, and great was the fall of it. (Matthew 7:24-27)

When you choose the Timeless Twenty Character Tools© and operate in the Green Zone, you will begin to experience a strength in all of your relationships because of your alignment with God. When you shoot for the Green Zone in each of your relationships you will lift up those around you rather than tear them down. When you lift up those around you by focusing on their needs rather than your own, you will build a solid foundation that people can depend on.

Having a solid foundation means that our loved ones and others can count on us to be consistent, constructive and supportive as we help them navigate the obstacles in their lives. They will be drawn to this strong foundation because it exudes the certainty and stability they desire. By our example, those around us will begin to understand that operating in the Green Zone is something they can do as well! Their foundation will mesh with ours and the relationships will become firm and unshakable.

Using the Timeless Twenty Character Tools© to build your personal foundation enables you to be a cornerstone in other foundations. When you walk in the Green Zone with God you can be a cornerstone for the foundation of your family, your church, your work or place of business and your social relationships.

Soon, you will notice that family members and others will begin to count on the consistency and strength that you offer in your relationship with them. They will appreciate you as a person who helps make their life stronger and healthier. As a family, you can be a source of inspiration and a cornerstone for your children and others as they build their own personal foundations. There is definitely value in that, and some people see that value as success. We see that value as the peace, contentment and satisfaction that you can only achieve when you use the Timeless Twenty

Character Tools© and walk with God in the Green Zone.

This is how we change the world for good! We start by changing our own world! We invite you to use the Times Twenty Character Tools© to build your personal foundation so that you can be a source of strength and inspiration for your families and those around you. As those around you notice the benefits that you have received from using the tools, *they will start choosing to use the tools in their lives as well*! It is contagious!

There are many people searching for ways to strengthen their lives and reconnect with God and those around them. We believe that when you choose to use the Timeless Twenty Character Tools© you are building your house on the rock so that when the rains fall and the floods come, you don't need to despair –you will weather the storm!

YOU WILL BE AN INSPIRATION TO OTHERS

"So encourage each other and build each other up, just as you are already doing."(1Thessolonians 5:11 NLT)

"Don't use foul or abusive language. Let everything you say be good and helpful, so that your words will be an encouragement to those who hear them." (Ephesians 4:29 NLT)

Have you noticed how some people shy away from or are uncomfortable with the fact that they are an inspiration to others? For some, it's quite natural but many of us don't see ourselves in a role of inspiring others.

It is also easy to believe that inspiring others should be left up to role models like sports figures, celebrities, successful business leaders and politicians. However, frequently these role models do not want to accept the responsibility of being in a position to inspire others. Some see it as irrelevant or as a burden too heavy or unreasonable to carry. It is sad, because that attitude alone is inspiring, just not in a positive way. It is actually inspiring people to be self-centered, negative and disconnected.

Inspiring, stimulating and motivating others is something that all of us do on a daily basis whether we realize it or not. In every relationship or interaction people are watching how we react to situations and receiving positive or negative inspiration from us. We can't control how others will perceive us but we do know they will be inspired, impacted or influenced from some aspects of our lives, whether it's positive or negative. When we choose to use the character tools in the Green Zone, we can rest assured that we are setting the example for others that God wants us to set.

The more we realize that we are inspiring people in a positive way when we use the Timeless Twenty Character Tools©, the more we will be motivated to continue to use the tools in all of our relationships. Inspiring people in a healthy way gives us a peace, contentment and a satisfaction that we are doing everything God wants us to do to make a positive difference in all of our relationships.

We invite you to join us as we walk with God in the Green Zone! We passionately believe in what we are telling you with every fiber of our being. We believe that the more you use each character tool and operate in the Green Zone, the stronger your relationship will be with God. Not only will you have a stronger relationship with God, but you will be *breathing* God into each day and every relationship in your life!

When you use the Timeless Twenty Character Tools© in your relationships you will find that you will become a *healthier friend* to your friends, a *healthier partner* to your spouse, a *healthier parent* to your children, a *healthier employee* to your boss and co-workers, a *healthier member* of your church or congregation, and a *healthier individual* within your community.

A good way to measure whether your relationships are getting healthier is to view them as a savings account. In any savings account, the goal is to make more deposits than withdrawals so that your account is never overdrawn. The same is true with your relationships. If we always strive to make more deposits (a symbol or a sign of our love and investment in the relationship) than withdrawals, the relationship (the account) will always be healthy. However, if our withdrawals (anytime we have a disagreement or say something hurtful) outnumber our deposits, our relationship (the account) will be unhealthy.

We want to walk with you in the green zone and offer you support as you learn to use these tools to build healthy relationships in your daily life. We invite you to join us at www.erikandtroy.com so that we can stay connected as we walk this walk together with God in the Green Zone.

We will be sharing positive, inspirational messages, podcasts and blogs to support and encourage you. We will also post information on upcoming workshops and seminars that you can attend. And, there will be a place for you to share your messages of hope and inspiration to others as you walk with God in the Green Zone.

Let this final piece of Scripture be our reminder to you that God's word guides us as we strive to have healthy relationships with everyone in our lives.

~WISDOM BESTOWS WELL-BEING~

My son, do not forget my teaching, but keep my commands in your heart,
for they will prolong your life many years and bring you peace and prosperity.
Let love and faithfulness never leave you, bind them around your neck,
  write them on the tablet of your heart.
Then you will win favor and a good name in the sight of God and man.
Trust in the Lord with all your heart and lean not on your own understanding;
in all your ways submit to him, and he will make your paths straight.
Do not be wise in your own eyes; fear the Lord and shun evil.
This will bring health to your body and nourishment to your bones.
Honor the Lord with your wealth, with the first fruits of all your crops;
then your barns will be filled to overflowing, and your vats will brim over with
new wine.
My son, do not despise the Lord's discipline, and do not resent his rebuke,
because the Lord disciplines those he loves, as a father the son he delights in.
Blessed are those who find wisdom, those who gain understanding,
for she is more profitable than silver and yields better returns than gold.
She is more precious than rubies; nothing you desire can compare with her.
Long life is in her right hand; in her left hand are riches and honor.
Her ways are pleasant ways, and all her paths are peace.
She is a tree of life to those who take hold of her; those who hold her fast will be
blessed.
By wisdom the Lord laid the earth's foundations, by understanding he set the
heavens in place;
by his knowledge the watery depths were divided, and the clouds let drop the dew.
My son, do not let wisdom and understanding out of your sight, preserve sound
judgment and discretion;
they will be life for you, an ornament to grace your neck.
Then you will go on your way in safety, and your foot will not stumble.
When you lie down, you will not be afraid; when you lie down, your sleep will be
sweet.
Have no fear of sudden disaster or of the ruin that overtakes the wicked,
for the Lord will be at your side and will keep your foot from being snared.

PROVERBS 3:1-26 (NIV)

ACKNOWLEDGMENTS

When we invited Jan Kraus (Troy's mother and Erik's mother-in-law) to join us, this project became stronger and more focused. While we focused on the concepts and the writing, Jan helped us with organizing, transcribing, and editing. We could not have written this book without her love and support.

Thank you to Drake Sauer (Troy's son-in-law) our graphics designer, for believing in our message and illustrating it through his creative and unique style.

We would also like to offer a special thank you to another member of our family, Carla Blowey, our editor. Carla (author of *Dreaming Kevin: The Path to Healing*) graciously agreed to complete the editing process for us. We're grateful for her skill and expertise in helping us complete the book.

Finally, we offer our heart-felt thanks to Pastor Karl Leuthauser, Senior Pastor of Grace Community Church in Montrose, Colorado. Pastor Karl provided sound theological guidance and inspiration that was vital to us in the process of completing *Victory Every Day*.

"When we unite, we can accomplish much more than we can alone. Joining forces can create a positive change and give us endless possibilities. Not only will we feel more connected to one another, but we will also feel stronger, more harmonious, and uplifted. Feeling a part of something greater than ourselves has been an experience that has enriched all of our lives."

~ **Erik S. Cooper & Troy Wehmeyer**

ABOUT ERIK & TROY

Erik S. Cooper   I am a licensed Marriage and Family therapist in private practice. I have been providing therapeutic services to individuals and families for over 23 years in southwestern Colorado. I am also the Clinical Director of a 16-bed, male, adolescent residential treatment facility. I have been married to my wife and best friend, Leslie, for 23 years, and we have two beautiful teenage daughters, Emma and Olivia.

I started my career and life path working with at-risk boys and their families at a residential treatment facility in inner city Denver. It was there that I realized my passion for helping adolescents and their families discover character and the sacredness of relationships. It was also at this treatment center that I met my wife, Leslie.

In my 23 years of private practice, I have worked with thousands of clients and their families, individually and in groups. I have noticed that we all share a universal desire for happiness and a connection to others. I believe this desire is the golden thread that connects us to one another. Happiness and connection can only be found in the present. Thus, my ultimate goal as a therapist is to inspire people to be present at all times.

Victory Every Day is full of practical and user-friendly tools designed to help you stay focused on the present. Throughout our 30-year relationship, Troy and I have practiced these tools again and again and are now confident that it is time to share them with you. This is our passion…this is our calling.

Troy Wehmeyer

I have been married to my high school sweetheart, Jeni, for 32 years. We have raised two happy children, Bryce and Breanne, who are now married and starting their own families. We are very excited about the upcoming birth of our first granddaughter, Lily, to Breanne and Drake!

I started my career in my early twenties working for a large corporation in the insurance industry. I was promoted from the field to be a part of the Regional Marketing Staff responsible for hiring, training and motivating agents in a 19 state region. This is where I met my Regional Vice President, Greg Knight, who would set a trajectory for my life that brought me to where I am today

Early in our relationship, Greg told me that I needed to be "a student of life". He explained that every person that I would come into contact with over the course of my life would be someone that I could learn something from. Greg encouraged me to look at each relationship and embrace all the things I see happening –the good and the bad alike. He said I should make a mental file cabinet in my mind with a "good" file for the good things that I see people do -the things that lift people up. These are things I will want to implement into my life. He also said that I should make a "bad" file for the bad things that I see people do –the things that tear people down. These are things that I definitely will not want to implement into my life.

Greg then gave me a final bit of inspiration that I have tried to instill into every aspect of my life. "People don't care how much you know. They want to know how much you care! This is something to remember with everyone you will deal with in your life from your family to your friends, co-workers, and people in your congregation, and those you meet every day on the street!" I took this advice to heart. Since then, I have tried to make every opportunity in my life be a building block that makes me a better person—regardless if the experience itself was positive or negative.

I excelled in the corporate world with Greg's philosophy and sage advice. However, in my late 20's, my wife, Jeni, and I were looking for a stable place to raise our family. We decided to move back home to Ogallala, Nebraska where we were surrounded and supported by extended family. This gave me an opportunity to be a sales/general manager with a start-up down comforter and textile manufacturing plant. Eventually, I realized that the corporate world was not for me and decided to become self-employed.

I explored a number of opportunities in the sales industry and ultimately became an independent sales contractor with Bear Graphics. We are a commercial print distributor/manufacturer with over 400 customers representing a 10 state area. Since 2000, Jeni and I have grown our business from $600,000 in sales to over $1,350,000 in 2015.

Making sure that our customers know how much we care in all aspects of our business has allowed it to thrive! My wife, Jeni, is our office manager and my mother, Jan, heads up our customer service department, and both Jeni and Jan are also in sales. I'm proud of the way they implement this philosophy in every aspect of their jobs. Jeni and Jan give our customers the assurance that they can always count on us, which in turn, makes us feel appreciated and successful!

Throughout my 30 years in the sales industry, I have learned that people have one universal desire and that is a desire for happiness and a connection to others. I realized early on that in each of my interactions, whether it be a family member, customer or a business associate, there is always an opportunity to connect with people and learn what I can do to lift them up in any way possible.

I have had thousands of interactions with people over the last 30 years, and with Erik's help, we have developed tools and techniques that have made me a more successful business owner, sales person, husband, father and friend! Erik and I have practiced these tools with great success and now, it is time to share them with you.

~NOTES ~

www.ingramcontent.com/pod-product-compliance
Lightning Source LLC
Chambersburg PA
CBHW080519030426
42337CB00023B/4568